TALES FROM THE PANTRY:

RANDOM RANTS & MUSINGS
OF A
STAY-AT-HOME MOM

Shari Owen Brown

ISBN-10: 0615515622

ISBN-13: 978-0615515625

PRINTED IN THE UNITED STATES OF AMERICA

ESTEP & FITZGERALD
LITERARY PUBLISHING

Table of Contents

"IF YOU DO NOT TELL THE TRUTH ABOUT YOURSELF, YOU CANNOT TELL IT ABOUT OTHER PEOPLE."

-VIRGINIA WOOLF

Dedicated to my Munchkins,
for without you, Mommy would be entirely too
sane to have embarked on this amazing adventure

The Pantry

Ooooh, the pantry. Aaaaah. It brings me such joy, and not because I love to cook. Even though I *do* love to cook. You see, my friends, the pantry was there for me in my time of need...my time of sorrow and utter desperation. El Desperado, that was me. El Desperado and Les Miserable all rolled into one. For I am a mother and the pantry was my solace. My haven. Protection from those that would do me harm...namely, my children.

Once upon a time, I had two kids. We moved into our new house when my son was born. Literally, the day before he was born we closed escrow on this house. Just as a sidebar...I do not recommend this. Ever. To infinity and beyond. NO moving when pregnant or with a baby. But I digress. Little did I know at the time, that this beautiful walk-in pantry would come to be so near and dear to me.

One day in sheer desperation, as I was contemplating shots of tequila at 8:36 a.m., I walked into the pantry to get something and I instinctually shut the door! Then I looked down and it was like an angel appeared before me and said, "Shari, LOOK! There's a LOCK ON THE DOOR!" At that moment, I knew. It was crystal clear to me: A mother had lived there before me.

God bless her foresight and 'out of the box' thinking. Because really, WHO has a lock on the INSIDE of their pantry?! ME, that's who! Jealous, much? Sorry, I shouldn't do that. I mean, we have just met for heaven's sake. Bad form, Shari! I shall wait until we are closer friends (maybe chapter four?) before I rub it in.

Regardless, my hope is to be an inspiration to all of the pantry dwellers out there. My dream is that I get you out of the bathrooms and hall closets, and into a place where the snacks are plentiful and the livin' is easy. The Pantry (I shall capitalize her for she deserves it) provides the perfect amount of muffling needed to take the edge off while still allowing you to know what the little hoodlums are up to! Not to mention all of the expired mac n' cheese and pumpkin pie filling you can discard.

Now you may be wondering, "Shari, why is motherhood so frustrating for you? Did you have children at a young age? Were you not prepared?" The answer is that I was old and prepared. I was, in fact, the last of my friends to have children. I mention this because that is where this all began.

It began in the middle of the night with my first child. It began as I was sitting there in complete tears with tape and tubes strapped to my boobs. If you don't know what I'm talking about...good for you! This medieval contraption was a bottle that hung around my neck, containing breast milk. The little tubes were taped to my boobs to try to train my baby to nurse more efficiently. Made little sense to me then. Makes even less sense to me now.

As I was pumping breast milk, feeding, wiping, washing

bottles and parts, laying down for twenty minutes only to be back up doing it all again, I couldn't help but curse the names of every mother-friend I have ever had! Every one of them! I contemplated calling them and screaming profanities at 2 a.m. for all of their lies, accusing their parents of having never been married. LIES, I tell you! Why is no one *talking* about this?! Is it just *me*? Can't be just me. What is this inhuman HELL that I have VOLUNTEERED for? It's not my fault! I didn't know! I wasn't given the right brochure! This parachute is a knapsack! GET ME OUTTA HERE!

Now is the time that I need to say to my non-mother friends, *you may need to sit down*. This may...*will*...get ugly. Like, for example, did you know that a newborn eats every two hours? Wasn't that shocking to me as I sat reading about it at five months pregnant. But then I hit the part that stopped me. In. My. Tracks. It is every two hours START TO START! START TO *START*, people! And some babies take forty-five minutes to eat! MINE DID!

Let me walk you through it. Baby wakes up at 2 a.m. to eat, finishing at 2:45. You change her diaper and put her back to bed at 2:55, then you get to go back to bed if you are one of the lucky ones. If you are *me*, Unlucky Luckerson, you will now need to use a breast pump to manually pump out more milk for twenty minutes. This helps generate a better milk supply, for those of us with babies who are 'inefficient suckers'. (Inefficient sucker. These words strike fear in the hearts of mothers everywhere.)

Now go rinse those breast pump parts so they are ready to roll for the next feeding. When will that be, you ask? Well, let's do the math...baby in bed at 2:55 a.m. + twenty minutes of pumping + five minutes of rinsing... you are back in your nice little bed at 3:20 a.m. and asleep by 3:30 a.m. IF you are lucky. And haven't yet *looked* at the clock to see that it is 3:30 a.m. Because if you look at the clock and SEE that it is 3:30 a.m. you will realize that you have EXACTLY thirty minutes to sleep until you get to do it all over again, which will bring on the adrenaline and the thought of 'hurry up and sleep, damn it!', which will ironically *prevent* you from sleeping.

This will happen around the clock. TWENTY-FOUR HOURS A DAY for what feels like eternity, but for most is hopefully only two months. When the baby is a little older, the feedings will stretch to every three to four hours and hopefully the baby will sleep a five-hour stretch at night. (Did you know that sleeping a five-hour stretch is considered 'sleeping through the night?' HA! Go ahead and cry. You need to. It's the right thing to do.) Of course, the baby's night starts at 6 p.m. so you have until 11 p.m. until the fit hits the shan and it starts all over again.

For you newbies out there, I'll give you a minute to catch your breath. All of the mothers are givin' me the hand to heaven 'testify' nod, am I right?! Nobody knows the trouble we've seen. The amount of tears seems endless at times, and THAT is with a healthy child! God bless all of the mothers who have to deal with a *sick* child! That kicks the stress into the stratosphere and I have nothing but absolute love and admiration for them.

One thing that motherhood has done for me is that it has taken all of the judgment out of me, except in cases of abuse and neglect. But now that's a fine line, isn't it? Some Judge Judys will ask if it is neglect to leave my screaming children wondering where Mommy has gone as I sit on the pantry floor stuffing my face full of bbq chips and graham crackers. (Hey! You grab what you have, people!) Some may say yes, it is neglectful. But where some see neglect I see protection! I am protecting my children from *myself*. My so-frustrated-that-I-could-throw-you-into-a-tree-and-walk-away self. Think of it as a Mommy time out.

We all do the best we can with what we have been given to work with. I have a newfound compassion for my fellow mothers because I know that we all have our less than stellar moments and God forbid it happens in public. We beat ourselves up enough without having our actions reflected back to us in the eyes of strangers. Bad enough to see the looks on our children's faces when we are screaming lunatics. Oh...okay, so maybe I am the only screaming lunatic...but I doubt it. I am convinced that mothers who talk the most about their wonderful children and wonderful lives are the ones that are the most full of shit. True story. This gig is HARD for EVERYONE! The work load, the fatigue, the never ending I'm-even-gonna-talk-and-cry-in-my-sleep-mom-so-you-don't-miss-me-ness of it all! I have felt many times like I am going to go crazy. And there is *no leaving* this job! Well, you could THINK about leaving but then you will turn on Oprah and see two little kids crying because their mother left them and hear how they cry themselves to sleep every night wondering why she didn't love them enough to stay and the little boy talks like Elmer Fudd and you find yourself bawling in the fetal position wanting to die for ever even having the thought enter your head. Hypothetically.

Motherhood is absolutely the most difficult thing I have ever done. I have had lots of jobs working all kinds of hours; doing everything from sales to serving drinks; all while working myself through college, eighteen units at a time. I considered myself a hard working person who had been in the trenches. I had survived the long nights and poverty and lived to tell the tale. I finally married the love of my life and at thirty-six the Lord blessed me with a beautiful and perfect baby girl. Life was good. Sure, I might be a little sleep deprived for a few weeks, but look at that *face*! Look at that cute little nose...wait, what?!...why is she crying?...no, I know they cry but WOW, that's really loud...what does she want? Oh, she wants to *eat*? Yes, I'm going to nurse. Oh, okay...OWWWW! SONOFA...IS THAT *RIGHT*?! Is it supposed to feel like...WHATTHE... Sweet MOSES...breathing...breathing. Okay, whew! Survived that one! Aaaaahhh...WAIT! I HAVE TO DO IT AGAIN ALREADY?! And so it goes. Add all of this to recovering from a c-section. Motherhood ain't for sissies!

Just the amount of time a baby takes up is astounding. It is all baby, all of the time. For those women (because men never seem to think this way) who think that a baby will bring you and your man closer, I give a resounding...HA! You best have your relationship on solid ground because there is NO TIME for gently requesting that your beloved bring you another diaper when his schedule allows. "DIAPER, STAT!" will be a common phrase when blowouts occur. And they will occur. Often. Out of one end or the other. One month in, you'll be lucky to find a shirt without a spit-up stain. True story.

And when you find yourself having the urge to smother your significant other in his sleep, rest assured that you are not alone. It is a rite of passage. Every mother has been there, unless she is highly medicated. Even with the best of husbands or fathers, the vast majority are not equipped to handle the stages of infancy. When you are at your wit's end because you have been up fourteen times in a five-hour period, and your man gives a loud grunt signifying his annoyance at being disturbed and having to, GOD FORBID, roll over, you are going to want to pound him in the head with a hammer. *Expect this.* Expect it, accept it, and start planning your revenge. JUST KIDDING!

(or am I?)

A woman, whether she has a job outside of the home or not, will do 80% of everything. Don't you shake your head at me! *It will happen.* Don't be fooled! We all say it won't happen to us! The toughest, most responsible man will be reduced to an eight-year-old boy in the face of nightly feedings. If he does decide to get up and help, be prepared for whining and moaning in the morning (and the entire next day, who are we kidding!?) the likes of which you've never seen. It's not sexy. I don't want to see it. Ever. It was better for me to just do it myself and then in the evening say, "I'm going to TARGET. *Alone*!"

It doesn't matter if you need something from Target or not. You will soon learn that Target is the haven for distressed mothers. We wander the aisles at night... alone...glazed and confused...savoring the sights and sounds, the smells of popcorn and the sweet chill of a cherry ICEE. We buy nail polish and tweezers, books we will never have time to read but we keep the dream alive, headbands and new ponytail holders for the Mommy 'do that is inevitable. We like to walk around and show off that at 6 p.m. that evening we actually got a *shower*! I know it isn't kind to brag, but sometimes you just gotta. Sure, our hair is still wet, but that's where the headband and ponytail holder come in. We have on a clean (sure it is stained, but what can ya do) shirt and our best sweat pants. We are hot and we know it.

This is the beginning of the loss of self. When your body and mind are so beyond exhausted that you are in survival mode. You are unable to care about anything other than sleep. Sounds romantic, I know. Makes you want to have six kids? Me too. And this is just with the *first* baby! Forget the fact that with the second baby there is no napping during the day with the baby. Hell no, because you've got a three-year-old who wakes at dawn and is up until 1 p.m. before she naps. You pray to your heavenly Father, the gods of sleep, and anyone that will listen, that the baby decides that 1 p.m. is a good time for a nap, too.

You do LOTS of math in your head when you have a baby. For example, toddler will nap at 1 p.m. so if I feed baby at 8:30 a.m., 10:30 a.m., and 12:30 p.m., then maybe they will BOTH nap at 1 p.m. and I can, too. You watch that clock like a hawk and pray to your own personal savior that the baby doesn't oversleep and screw up your beautiful master plan. Let me tell you now, nine times out of ten it ain't gonna work out. It sucks. It all sucks. You will be tired and irritable and wonder what ever happened to the happy-go-lucky girl with tons of energy and a gleam in her eye. I'll tell you what happened...she fell in love and then motherhood kicked her in the nads.

It won't be forever. This is what they tell me. This is my mantra as I am lying prone in The Pantry. Best advice I ever got was that everything with kids is a phase. It won't last long. Oh sure, it's gonna feel like an eternity, but once they are done with the refusing-to-latch phase and screaming to the point where you are now sweating and these little suckers become as slippery as a wet piglet so getting a good latch is now next to impossible, and you are using a nursing cover to be discreet but you have now found yourself completely under the cover yourself with only the top of your hair sticking out because piglet won't stop wiggling and you can't see to get the latch, they will eventually move on to an equally enjoyable phase. The fun just never stops.

With all of this truth being told, it is time to share a peeve o' mine. As mothers, myself included, when we are venting and trying to make sense of this primal urge we had to procreate and cause ourselves such misery, we feel the need to qualify every statement with the obligatory "I love my children, don't get me wrong!"

I would like to start a national campaign to rid ourselves of this statement. OF COURSE, WE LOVE OUR KIDS! We would take a bullet and knock out a bully for looking sideways at our kids. We shouldn't feel the need to say it when we are dealing with difficult circumstances for which we often feel ill-equipped to handle. You will never grow as much as a human being as you will when you have children. You will never love something so completely as you will love your kids. Still doesn't mean you don't want to run screaming from the building, but then you remember the Oprah episode and Elmer Fudd and you take a breath or have a good breakdown and decide to stay another day.

All Because a Girl Had to Pee

January 3

Nothing. I got nothing...maybeeeeeee...nope. Nada.
Kicking off 2011 with a bang, I tell ya! Maybe there's just a
log jam of rants. Watched *Ax Men* last night and learned
that logs get jammed and clog up the process. Thinkin' I
have a log jammed. I get little trickles of thought and
inspiration, but the big gushers seem to be few and far
between. Probably because I've just got too much jammed
up in there. I know I've got a log marked 'Christmas Tree'
because although I took all the decor down four or five
days ago, this tree is still sitting here. Staring at me. With

its lights on. I mean, it's right here next to me. Staring. Cuz to have a tree sitting, staring, WITHOUT lights on is just sad. This is a tad less sad. But it's like he's saying, "Get off your lazy butt and take me DOWN already! This is getting embarrassing!" I know this is what he's saying. Stop looking at me! Stupid tree! I'll turn those lights out. Don't think I won't!

The reason this tree has not come down yet is because of log #2, which is cooking. Since we had zero plans for the New Year and since my mom is laid up with a broken leg, I decided to be festive and cook some fun stuff. So that involved menu planning, shopping, cooking, cleaning and delivering. Mix into that logs #3 and #4 which are Sissy and Bubba. Had to take care of them in betwixt and between. Okay, then there's the laundry log...the "Kid's store mismarked several pairs of their leggings as size six when they are really only a four or five so I have to go through, measure and return them" log, the "it's Sunday and hubby has the kids so I better get out while the gettin's good" log, the "Sissy is in school and baby is napping so you better keep your New Year's resolution and blog more even though you haven't had a shower yet" log. Let's see, what else...oh, the "I have a new Kindle that I love and

have no time to read like I want to because I have all of
these logs" log, the "Sissy wet the bed last night so we have
emergency laundry that has to cut ahead of all the other
laundry" log and in the meantime I realized that there's a
new log today marked, "My new everyday sweater that I
love is DRY CLEAN ONLY which does NOT make it an
everyday sweater anymore!" I am a mother, dammat!!! We
do not DO 'dry clean only'! Can I get an amen!?!

See, told ya there was a rant in there somewhere. This is a
testament to the fact that I can go on and on with
nothing...about nothing...to infinity and beyond. Maybe in
the process of this nothingness I have unjammed a log or
two. Blog is done, now off to change laundry and shower!
But first I have to go slap this tree.

January 8

Now, I love my husband...don't get me wrong. BUT, what
is the dealio with greeting cards these days?! I am
BEYOND frustrated. I go to get him a birthday card and
heaven help me, but I'm in that freakin' aisle for thirty
minutes! Every card says, "To the man I love...", yeah...
okay, I do love him, but what is this...a Tella

Novela?! "For the one who makes my life complete...", "I never knew love could feel this way..." (Okay, that one is kinda true cuz sometimes it really blows), "If someone would have told me that in the ocean of love I would meet someone as great as you ..." Oh dear LORD, I'm nauseous over here! Can't you just say, "Hey buddy, love ya more than my luggage, and I'm forever grateful that I don't have to go on any more loser dates. If you could see it in your heart to keep the farting to a minimum, I'd be forever grateful. Happy Birthday!" As I was talking to these ridiculous cards at Target, I noticed some young twenty-somethings picking out 'Love' cards. I'm sure I burst a few bubbles as I'm repeatedly saying, "OhPUUHHHLEEEZ!" with a fussy baby in the cart and a four-year-old singing her version of Preschool Musical. Well, consider it my Public Service Announcement. Someone has to break it down for these ladies. It ain't all hearts and roses. Most often it's butts and sippy cups. IN that order.

Sidebar: I was shopping at the mall last week and the salesgirl was about twenty-two years old. She was talking about her boyfriend who only liked to travel with the amount of stuff he could fit into his backpack. (I'm thinking, "What, is he NINE?! That's not a man, that's a boy!) She was trying to convince him to go to either Hawaii or to Italy with her. THEN Salesgirl says, "Yeah, I told him I'd pay because otherwise we'd never go. He would never spend money like that on me." That's when my mouth flew open. As if it was separate from my body. I jumped my little (shut up!) self, right into that girl's beeswax and said, "Aaah, little tip from one who dated for seventeen years before finding Mr. Right...if he won't spend money on you NOW, he never will. If you want to dish out that kind of money, take one of your girlfriends with you. You will have a much better time and you will never regret it." Wish you could have seen the look on her face. It's like the clouds parted and she saw the light for the first time! And then, like Spiderman fading into the night, I was gone. My work there was done. Now back to our regularly scheduled program...

I truly think that the people who wrote these cards are not married. That should be a requirement. And I'm talking married for like five years, at least! If you've only been married for a couple of years then you can work in the Engagement Department or in Newlyweds. You cannot work in the Anniversary Department! And I believe that Mr. Greeting Card needs to separate the Anniversary

Department into smaller divisions, one being cards for couples married less than five years...let's call it the *Isn't Love Grand* Department.

Next, we have the section for couples who have been married for five to ten years with young children, entitled the *Love is Great but I'd Rather Sleep* department (This is my dept. :)) For those who have been married from ten to twenty years, there is the *Who Does a Girl Gotta Sleep With To Get Some HELP Around This House!?!* Department. And for those fantastic couples who have made it twenty plus years we have the *I'm Too Tired To Tell You You're An Idiot* Department ~cue music~ ...there is loooooooove....therrrrrre...iiiiiissss...loooooooooooove. (It's okay to say it out loud...I'm sweet.)

January 30

I peed my pants. I literally. peed. on. myself. Whomp, there it is. Me, in all my glory. This is what my life has come to. Two degrees, a small business owner, wife and mother of two, and now I will only be known as The Urinator. I accept defeat WORLD! YOU WIN! I peed the fight right out of me. How did I find myself in such a situation, you ask? Well, pardon the pun but it all started because I was pissed. Literally and figuratively. Let's take a look back, shall we?...~cue wobbly screen and Mike Meyers~ "biddily-doo, biddily-doo, biddily-doo".

So there I was, waiting on the refrigerator repairman for visit # 14. I. kid. you. not. And if you are saying, "Shari! There's a lemon law! Insist on a new refrigerator!" then I need you to give me your address so that I can come over and punch you in the face. Don't worry, I won't stay long. I'll just ring the bell, you'll answer, PUNCH, back in my car, and I'm gone. I do not have the strength to go into the entire story with you, just like I didn't have the strength to tell repairman # 8 what was wrong with my fridge. I told him, "You are not Kevin. Kevin is my repairman. He knows what is wrong. Last time they sent Robert. Robert had to call Kevin because he knows what is wrong. Robert didn't know. He called Kevin. Robert and Kevin spent two and a half hours trying to fix it. Needed another part. Kevin said he would come back because he knows what's going on. You do not. I will not tell you what is going on for fear of flying into a rage that I may never recover from. I'm sure your family loves you and will miss you when you are gone. If I have to repeat my story to one more person, that person may not live to tell the tale. Save yourself and go get KEVIN!!!" Of course then he said that Kevin could come tomorrow (I'M NOT WASTING ONE MORE DAY!) and it was already 6:30 p.m ....my window was 1-5 p.m. Which is why he was here at 6:30 p.m. They enjoy showing up ninety minutes past the window. I know this. I have done extensive research on this in the form of scheduling FOURTEEN VISITS!!!! Now in Kevin's defense, his company has only been on six of the fourteen calls. The previous visits were split between four different companies. None of them spoke English, only Russian. I, unfortunately, do not speak Russian. It's not that I wouldn't LIKE to speak Russian, it just never came up. As a child, had I have known that someday Russian would be imperative to the repair of my appliances; I would have sought books, tutors, scholars, to aid me in my quest. But coulda, shoulda, woulda. I have now come to discover that it isn't that Moscow has a huge billboard that says, "Go to America, Fix Appliance". It's that four brothers own four repair companies. They share one warehouse and start all of their companies with the letter A. That way, when you Google or look them up in the phone book, their company is at the top. (Sorry, I'm having a hard time writing right now because for some reason, when thinking of Russia I want to talk in short, choppy sentences. Like...come fix fridge. Fridge no work. Piece of crap. What is borscht? Is it just me?...oh no, wait...Just me. That's better.)

Back to the pee. SO, I've completely forgotten where I was in the story and I'm too damned tired to read what I wrote so here goes...window is 1 p.m.-5 p.m. At 2:30 p.m., I get a call that he'll be here closer to 5 p.m. Of course he will. ~rolls eyes~ Now this screws up my program because I needed to go to my mom's house to do laundry. (WHOLE OTHER OPRAH! Brand new "AprilTag" washing machine is on the fritz, too! Serenity NOW!) AND mom was going to make dinner for me and the kids since hubby was working late. Scratch all that, because now I have to make dinner for the kids and have no clue when hubby is going to get his panties washed. (He doesn't really wear panties, that I know of. I just use that phrase when I'm mad. For example, "Don't get your panties in a bunch," "Calm down, you're running around here like your panties are on fire!" It calms me. It's an outlet. What can I say?) So it's a little after 5:00 p.m. and I finally have two seconds to pee. I've had to pee for over an hour, but I've got two little kids so it's not always an option. Wouldn't you know, JUST as I start to go...the phone rings. It's the repairman, I just know it! If I don't answer, he won't come! O.M.G. I try to stop peeing...wth?...can't stop...too much pee...must get phone...STOP PEEING!!!!...I grab tissue...baby's in the way...MOVE Bubba!!!...OMG!!!...Third ring... SONOFA$^%&*..."HELLO?!"...this is when he tells me that he is Peter, NOT Kevin, and I go into my whole "Who do I have to sleep with to get Kevin here ON TIME?!" spiel. (It was a dark day, my friends. I'm not gonna lie to you.) And now I'm thinking...why am I wet?...what's wet?...there's wetness...all while having this convo with Peter. Then I realize O.M.G. Did I just pee myself? What THE...where's Bubba? What's that noise?...OMG! Bubba is in the bathroom, splashing in the toilet. Water is everywhere. Or is that pee? O.M.G. PLEASE, somebody knock me out. I want to be unconscious RIGHT NOW. Still having convo with Peter...washing Bubba... changing MY OWN pants...cuz I peed myself, ya know... still having convo. And now I'm shaking because I'm so pissed. HA! Yeah. That phrase takes on a whole new meaning.

Thank God for mothers because I called my mom, she

came and got the laundry, and took it to her house. Peter showed up at 6:30 p.m., not knowing what sort of hell he was walking into. Fortunately for him, I had my breakdown before he got here and was in some altered state of numbness by the time he showed up. Post Traumatic Pee Disorder. PTPD, for those in the industry. So he installs the part while telling me that he's never done this before. All I could muster was a "that's nice." At least I still had my wits about me enough not to finish with ..."I peed my pants."

February 9

Dost thou 'tweet'? I do not. I try, but I get too confused. WTH. I cannot understand this thing! I get the concept, and I am really not that dense in the technology department, but what with all of the '#' and '@RT's', I just get lost. The most time I have ever spent on there was when I was following a live tweet during a reality show. Even then I was getting lost trying to figure out where the comments were that they were responding to. But one thing that stuck with me, and actually brings me great joy, is the '#'. I had someone explain it to me and apparently, if you are searching the Twitter site for something in particular, like comments about chocolate souffle', you would type #chocolatesouffle and those comments will appear. If you want other people to be able to search your comments about chocolate souffle', you would type #chocolatesouffle after you reviewed a recipe, visited a restaurant, jumped on the scale. "I gained four pounds this week! #chocolatesouffle" :)

Let me tell you, lots of fun to be had with '#'. #thisisahoot. See what I just did there? :) Why does this bring me such joy, I ask you! #wherehaveyoubeenallmylife. I just can't stop. #Shariisabouttogetannoying. Try it. You'll like it! #Don'tknowwhatyouaremissing.

It is kind of like the subliminal message that you want to convey but don't want to come right out and say. For example, you are at the soccer field and Gossip McGossipson is running her mouth. So you tweet, "People need to grow up and stop gossiping. It isn't nice and sends the wrong message to our children. #bitchgonnagetafootupherass." :) Aaaaahhhh, that feels good, doesn't it? I recommend doing it as often as possible!

Every Girl Needs
a Pit Crew

February 11

I discovered something that is helping me deal with my...
shall we say...issues. SWINGS! No, not baby swings! But
I can see why you'd go there with all of my talk of hiding in
The Pantry. I'm talking BIG SWINGS! Like at the park.
The kind that you watch your kids on all the time but never
actually sit in yourself. Well let me tell you, brothers and
sisters, THIS is what we are missing!!! I accidentally
hopped on the other day while at the park and decided to
swing. I went higher and higher, and with each pump of
my legs I started feeling something I haven't felt in

YEARS...pure joy. Don't laugh! I am serious. Pure. Joy. And I never was much of a swing person per se, but there is something about that motion. I'm telling you, my chakras, karma, mojo...they were all singin'! I don't know if it was because on the swing you are totally in the moment. I don't know if it is the movement. But I am telling you, get your ass to the park! If only they would make adult sized swings. HOW FUN WOULD THAT BE?! We need an adult park with big honkin' slides and merry go rounds and SWINGS! Screw PROZAC! To hell with ZOLOFT! We need playgrounds! NO KIDS ALLOWED! MASSIVE wedgies to the parent who even THINKS about bringing their kids there! Our juice boxes will be very large...filled with a nice Pinot. No shoes allowed and screaming encouraged! Move over, Dr. Phil! Depression be damned! We will play and sing and scream and toast to the funk we're in, knowing that better days are around the corner! Think of it as a community support group. No need to speak your name, no need to comb your hair, or to say that you have children who do not listen or give a rat's patoot that you are a slave to their every need. We know. We can see the look of desperation in your eyes and we recognize it as our own. We are here for you, Brother...

Sister...Friend. :) I'll push you if you'll push me!
#swingersrock

February 20

I am starting to wonder if I will be sticky for the rest of my
life. I never really paid much attention to how often I was
sticky before having kids. Probably because I wasn't ever
sticky. Or if I was sticky, I would wash my hands and be
done with it for another year or so. But after having
children I find that sticky has become a way of life. A
lifeSTYLE, if you will. For I am forever sticky...gummy...
tacky...and not in that tacky "I'm wearing teal toe nail
polish" kind of way. (I mention that because I just made
this poor choice today. Not sure what I was thinking. I
think I got caught up in my imaginary "Carrie Bradshaw"
life again. Shari Bradshaw, if you will. I have a closet full
of clothes, shoes, and handbags that were purchased when
I was under this influence. Then I come back to reality
and find my teal toes sticking to the floor.) FOR THE
LOVE OF GOD! Where does this crap come from?!
Raisins? Granola Bars? Cheerios? Juice?

I wash these children. I swear that I do. Constantly

washing. Wiping. Rinsing. Can't seem to keep up. And when I do get MYSELF cleaned up, it is inevitable that within ten minutes I will touch something or step in something that I missed. It's like they do it to taunt me. Like little sticky gremlins who are trying to see how much more it will take before I end up hiding in the pantry in the fetal position. #Imightnevercomeout #notabadmomjuststucktothefloor .

My favorite part is when Daddy gets home and in his most shocked voice says, "Why is the refrigerator sticky?!" I'm breathing...I'm breathing...and in scary whisper I say, "Be...cause...IIIIIIIIII AMMMMM STICKYYYYYYYY!!!!!!"

March 1

I've said it before and I'll say it again, people. If you allow your cat to get up on your kitchen counter, they will inevitably sit on said counter. Am I the only one making the connection here? You now have cat butt on your kitchen counter. So later, when you lay an apple on the counter while you get a paper towel, you now have...Cat Butt Apple. When you lay your hand on the counter, then reach for your sandwich...Cat Butt Sandwich. Unless you

Clorox that son of a gun every half hour (because you don't know how often that cat puts his butt up there when you aren't looking!), you are eating cat butt. It's sick, sick, sick, and there is no reason a CAT should be allowed on the kitchen counter. Just my thoughts on the matter. Cat butt! Cat butt! Cat butt! Blech! #catbuttblows

March 16

Today I would like to express myself through a poem. An 'ode', if you will. (I'm a big fan of ode's. :))

Ode to a Ceiling Fan

Oh ceiling fan, high up in the air,
Didn't know you were spinning, forgot you were there.

You do me the favor of keeping me cool,
When you wacked at my fingers, I felt like a fool.

When one has a stature, as tall as mine
You keep me in check when I get out of line.

Raising my arms to put on my top

You inform in a hurry, your blades will not stop.
So I bid you respect, give you your due,
Now I'm off to get Band-Aids for my little boo-boo.
Amen.
#imtoostupidtolive

March 26

Zoo + Movies = ZOOVIES!

Sounds fun, huh?! I THOUGHT SO! I was so excited!
Thought my four-year-old daughter would be, too. But
here is something that I never expected with motherhood:
I am more excited about taking Sissy to do kid-stuff than
she is! I never thought my little one would turn into
Debbie Downer. Who is this kid and WHO IS HER
MOTHER!? Surely not me! I love to go places and do fun
stuff, and LORD knows those moments are few and far
between with an additional baby. I always thought I would
look forward to kid-stuff outings and seeing them through
the eyes of my child. Pbbbtttthhhhh! (that was the best
raspberry I could muster) Anyone have any kids they want
to lend me? The latest outing started out fine, a one-hour

drive to Santa Barbara with no traffic to attend "Zoovies" (Movies at the zoo!) Sissy was asking for ice cream so I got her a little bit for the ride there. Fun, right?! Go MOM! Half way there I get the first ever "Are we there yet?" Oh geez! Should have been my first clue. But she rallied and was super excited when we pulled into the parking lot. We had a great time looking at the animals on our way to the grassy area where the movie was to be shown. I paid a little extra so she could jump in the bounce house. Again...YAY MOM!

We headed up to the grass and that's when it started... there was the faintest stench of animalness. Sissy plugged her nose immediately and made a squishy face, saying "Bom, ids dinky." Yeah, yeah, kid. I know. You'll get used to it. "No Bom, id don't dmell dood." I was PRAYING for a breeze! (and let me take this moment to tell you that it was the most PERFECT Santa Barbara evening at the beach that you could imagine! It was 72 degrees at 8 p.m!) I tried to distract her. They had beanie babies! Do you want one? "Do dhanks." (still holding her nose. Sheesh!) What kid doesn't want a Beanie Baby?! So I got one to take home to Bubba.I found a great spot and got set up. I had the blanket, the chair, the quilt, licorice-the works! Kid still won't let go of her nose. FINALLY we get a slight breeze and she seems to forget about it. Then she wants popcorn. Didn't want popcorn when there wasn't a line. Now, suddenly, the urge for corn is overwhelming her. Okay, off to stand in line. We finally get the $6 popcorn in a collector tub, (give me a break), and head over to stand in the drink line. Takes for-EVER! It is almost our turn and she tells me she doesn't want the popcorn. She hasn't had ONE BITE yet. Doesn't want it. (I controlled my urge to dump the whole bucket right there in the trash!) That was the whole point of the drink, to wash down the corn. So NOW I'm pissed! Okay, no corn? Then no drink! We leave the line and go sit down. She is crying of course, saying she's thirsty. Well, the movie is ninety minutes long so she can deal until we get to the car. I probably should have gotten the drink, but at the zoo, they don't have lids or straws and I didn't want to deal with balancing that drink if it wasn't really necessary. And without the corn...NOT NECESSARY!

Movie starts, she's acting happy, sitting in my lap. There's a HUGE screen on the lawn, weather is perfect, seats are great, sun is setting, and I'm feeling good! Forty-five minutes into the movie..."I want to go home." WTH?! I'm zero to pissed in two seconds. Fine! I packed that crap up so fast it made her head spin and we were OUTTA THERE! Freakin' kid ruined my fun! I asked if she had fun..."yes"...Do you want Mommy to bring you back for another movie next week?..."No, you can bring Bubba." $*%&@

Now she usually is in bed around 8:30 p.m., but most nights she'll sing in her bed until at least 9:15 or 9:30. Some nights she's not in bed until 9:00 and then I still hear her around 10:00. So I thought, big whoop, we sit and watch a movie until 9:30/9:45 and she snoozes on the way home. Well apparently, she is sleepier in the evening than I am aware. She fell asleep in the car half way home. Oh, after downing half of a bottle of water. So I guess she *was* thirsty, but I'm telling you, in my state of mind, if I would have got that drink and she would have refused it...let's just say we wouldn't even have stayed for the opening credits. Mama don't play!

So there you have it, in all its glory. Everything about the Zoovies is fantastic, unless you are my daughter. If you have the means, you should check it out! I'm still holding out hope for Bubba, but in my experience with Sissy? That kid ruins every fun thing I ever try to do for/with her. Mama needs an aspirin after just TELLING that story! Thank you and goodnight.

April 2

I have this thing with tires. My entire life I have been plagued with flat tires and all sorts of tire issues. Ask my dad, it goes waaaaayyy back to my little bicycle with the flower basket and big orange flag on the back. (That flag is still a sore spot for me so leave it alone!) So today I got the kids ready and as I was loading them in the car, I noticed that my right rear was flat (don't be intimidated by my use of 'right rear.' It comes from many years of Nascar, so don't beat yourself up over it. I'm a professional.) CRAP! Well, as I was walking back in the house to tell the hubster, I noticed something...something that brought me great joy with a side order of pride...don't ask me why, but it did. I went from "Oh crap, this sucks!" to "Hey honey! Come look what I did!"

There was a half of a pair of scissors jammed into the tire. But that was not what was so impressive. The other half of the scissors were stuck IN THE WHEEL WELL, PEOPLE! How cool am I?! Jealous, much? Now hubby will tell you that 'officially' he was aggravated...until he saw the VISION. I caught a glimpse of that little smile. He tried to hide it but I could see it, plain as day. That was pride, my friend...pure pride.

It is but a symbol, given to me from the gods, of my recent mental struggle over how to get Sissy's and my hair cut with this little boy in tow. It is as if the universe is saying to me, "Yes, Shari, haircuts suck!" or maybe just a simple "SCREW THE HAIRCUT!" I am at peace. Namaste'.

I should tell you that I once had an AAA tire man tell me that the pliers I ran over, that shaped themselves into a perfect "L," were the strangest thing he had seen in twenty years. ~heavy sigh~...wish I had his number...

And then there was the time that all four wheels were stolen off of my new Honda Accord and I woke up to find my car sitting on blocks. True story. Try calling for a tow on that one! Kept having to explain to the insurance guy that..."I HAVE NO WHEELS! How can you tow me?!" Had to get a ride to Honda, buy four new WHEELS (not just tires!), take them back to my car, and THEN call the tow man to put them on the car. I was amazed they could get the jack under the car! Where's my pit crew when I need them?! #juniornationforever

Customer Service My Ass

April 27

Okay, what the hell is going on in this world?! Because
something is DEFINITLEY going on! Why is it more
common to have something screwed up than to have it
done right? I'm talking getting cheese on your sandwich
when you specifically said no cheese (because your special
diet frowns on cheese, not because you don't like cheese,
you are just forbidden from it)...giving you REAL Coke
when you ordered diet...children's leggings that SAY they
are a size six but really they are a size five, so as your
daughter is walking into her classroom and she bends

down to pick something up, you see baby butt crack. You try to return them and the store confirms that yes, they are marked wrong, but no, they won't take back the array of tops that you bought to match the leggings because the tops aren't mismarked. So now, you have no bottoms and your daughter is built like a pole so she can't wear jeans because she is too tall and now you have all of these tops and no bottoms. Okay, that one is likely just me. But what about ordering something through the mail and it arrives broken? Or getting boots with two right feet? Or charging you for the $80 pedicure when your gift card CLEARLY STATED IT WAS $80 FOR A MANI/PEDI so then you still owe $35 ~faints~

Can't just be me. Seems as though this is becoming an epidemic. Either nobody cares, or they are all stupid. Which is it? One of my Facebook friends recently made a wish that stupidity was painful. Wouldn't. That. Be. AWESOME!?!!!!! Omg! I would LOVE that. I could sit outside of the local teen punk clothing store and watch all of these kids saying, "Ow...Ow...OOWWWWW!!!" I could call my cable company and hear, "Due to a large volume of ...OW!...calls, wait times are...OW! ...longer than usual... OWW! Your call is very...OWW!...important to us. CRAP!

OW!" That would bring me joy. Because really, who are the stupid people hurting now? ME! Enough, I say!

To the preschool teacher that serves my child her snack at 8:30 a.m. when she walks in the door... ENOUGH! To the drive-thru person who speaks so fast I have no clue what they are saying and NO, I DON'T WANT A YUMBO YACK, ENOUGH! To the sales clerk who wipes her nose with her hand and then proceeds to hand me my change, ENOUGH! To the receptionist at the doctor's office who acts like she's the one who went to medical school instead of smokin' her cigs behind the Jiffy Mart trying to get someone to buy her beer, ENOUGH! I'm taking a stand, people! I will not dumb myself down. Raise the standards! Insist that life rise up to meet you! I am sick and tired of battling and arguing with people who just don't seem to have the sense that God gave a goose! TELL ME it's not just me!

May 9

There is currently a phenomenon taking place across America and your roving reporter is here to bring it to you! Don't be fooled by media propaganda! The recession is apparently all in our imaginations, because although "my call is very important" to these companies, they are all "currently experiencing high call volumes and longer wait times." Who are these companies, you ask? Well, apparently it is EVERYONE! EVERY flingin' flangin' company from here to the Appalachians is experiencing 'high flippin' call volume'! Phone company, cable company, refrigerator repairman, and even freakin' infomercial hotlines! So business must be good, huh? Since everybody seems to be so busy! Or are the millions who are out of work sitting at home on the phone calling these companies because they are lonely and need someone to talk to? Here's a thought...how about HIRING some of these out of work Americans to man your phones?! Seems to be a desperate need, unless you think it is good customer service to keep a woman on HOLD FOR TWENTY-FIVE MINUTES WHO HAS TWO LITTLE KIDS?! Oh, and don't think I didn't write your name down MR. DAVID, aka 'Customer Care Specialist'! I got your specialist right here!

I'm breathing...I'm breathing...release...relent... relinquish...recoil...rebar...wth?... reheat?...okay, moving on! I'm not an idiot. (Shut up!) I know they are not really experiencing a 'high volume of calls.' They've just laid off 80% of their staff and are leaving the normal volume of calls up to Skippy and Mr. David, Customer Care Specialist. So just don't lie to me. That's what ticks me off! When that freakin' recording says OVER and OVER that I'm special, they love me, the sun rises and sets on me... blah, blah, blah, it makes me want to HURT SOMEONE. Meanwhile, I've got a crick in my neck from wiping butts and making peanut butter sandwiches with the phone in my ear! I would much rather hear the truth: "Due to the fact that business is currently sucking, we've got two teenagers with attitudes who'd rather be anywhere but here (and have no authority to solve your problems) answering our phones because we only have to pay them in sandwiches and juice boxes. We've asked them to please give a crap and speak as though they don't have a mouth full of marshmallows and are on triple the legal dose of Valium, but they are teenagers, what can ya do?! Please rest assured that when business improves, we will hire even more teenagers because, let's be honest, they are cheap and we really want to make as much money as possible at the customer's expense. Thank you for your patience, now go shit in a hat."

May 12

You wanna piss off a mom? Give her some french fries hot out of the fryer! There is not a mom out there who doesn't know what I am talking about! You decide to treat the kids...be the hero...you know, try to be dad for a few minutes. So you hit the drive-thru, wait for what seems like an eternity while listening to your restless two-year-old scream and his sister yell at him to stop screaming, knowing that quiet bliss is but moments away...And then they give you the bag.

As you sit it on your lap and feel the pangs of second-degree burns, you know this is NOT gonna be good. Nothing like sitting in the parking lot with 60-degree temps outside, and the a/c blasting as you hold up french fries to the vent as those mother effers are burning the flesh right off of your fingers. Enduring the confused looks of men who drive by. LOOK AWAY, BUDDY. YOU HAVE NO IDEA WHAT IT MEANS TO BE A MOTHER. The sheer depth, range and scope of ridiculous crap that we have to deal with is a constant bombardment on the brain of creativity. How to get through the day with the least amount of screams and tantrums...and the kids act up sometimes as well. (ba-dum-BUM!)

But seriously, fresh is NOT GOOD when it comes to children. Give me the fries that have been sitting out for ten minutes or so. Nothing thrills me like a lukewarm nugget! I am ashamed to admit that I know not to go through the drive-thru at 11:30 a.m. EVERYTHING is hot! If you are sitting there judging me, then you are a) not a mother, b) you have a huge support system, or c) just a judgmental b-hole who needs to spend a few hours with my youngest. I know, you don't have to say it...I'm sweet.

May 30

The other day I was waiting in line at the local farm, veggies in hand, two kids in tow. I've got Granola Gwen in front of me and Magilla Gorilla behind me (referring to her MASSIVE biceps and bulging veins. This woman does WAY too much working out.) I found myself between these two ladies and the irony was not lost on me.

You know those women with the nasally voices who insist on calling to their unruly children at full volume?! "Phiiiiiillliiiip! I'm leeeeeeeeeaviiiiiiiiing. I'm goooooooooooiiiiiiiiiiing. Good-byyyyyyyyyyyyyye Phiiiiiiiiiillllllllliiiiiiiiip." Over and over and over. The rest of us are cringing and Phiiiiiiiiiliiiiiiiip is far away and couldn't care less. It is obvious that he's used to this and it means nothing to him. This lady was pulling out every child psychology trick in the book. Ridiculous! Go grab that brat by the arm and PUT HIS ASS in the car! That will be the day that I'm making a complete ass out of myself in a public place. (I prefer to do it privately, thank you very much.)

This kid was about nine years old. I can just see when he hits thirteen. I can hear it now: "All of a sudden he's not listening. He just doesn't do what he's told. I don't know what happened. Must be the teen years." UGH! No, he's been ignoring you his whole life, now he's just bigger! If you can't make them mind you when they are small, what makes you think you will be able to do it when they are bigger? My peanut gallery opinion is that if you don't set the ground work before they are three or four, you're done. Toast.

Take a Photo, Take a Bullet. You Choose.

June 5

Can we talk for just a minute? Just between us chipmunks? (Don't ask. If you don't know me by now, let me just explain that sometimes there is no explanation for what flies out of my mouth.) Anywho...I have to say that I am honestly sick and tired of seeing articles, books, and shows about 'Women Learning to Love Themselves', and 'Finding the Beauty Within.' It's not that I'm against women learning these things, I guess I just wish it wasn't necessary. Do we not know that beauty is within? Why don't men have these problems? Like women don't have enough to deal with, without having to worry about this? Can't we all just put on our Big Girl Panties and try to be good people and kind to our fellow neighbor, and the other crap be damned? Maybe it comes from being a chipmunk (there it is again) but I am just so sick of hearing about it. I have had days when I have felt down, of course. But it just seems like an epidemic these days. It must sell lots of magazines and give the talk shows great ratings or I guess they wouldn't talk about it so much.

I remember when I was in the sixth grade and I was starting to see the dynamics happening between boys and girls. I knew I wasn't one of the pretty girls. I mean, I wasn't homely, but definitely not a head turner. Several of my friends got a ton of boy attention, and I didn't, except to be friends. I remember thinking to myself, "Okay Shari, looks aren't your thing, so you better work on that personality!" I vividly remember thinking this. So I did. And I knew I was smart. So I decided to work on the positives and accept what I had to work with. I had a friend who wasn't the best looking girl, but people were drawn to her because she was so much fun and smiled all the time. Bingo! That would be me! I didn't attract all of the boys, but I believe I attracted the ones that mattered, and in the end, isn't that what's important?

Here's what I wonder...when we have moments that we aren't feeling so great about ourselves, what if we went out and did something nice for someone else? I'm not trying to get all Pollyanna on your ass, but I wonder if it is possible to be depressed about your own life when you're volunteering at a homeless shelter, battered women's home, or donating food and clothing. This is an honest question, I'm not trying to make anyone feel bad about themselves, FOR HEAVEN'S SAKE! Wouldn't THAT be counterproductive?! But that brings up another thought: Why should what someone says make somebody feel bad about themselves, unless it is directly addressed at that person? Like if someone said, "Shari, you are an idiot." Offensive. But if someone said, "All writers are idiots," I'm not offended by that because I know I'm not an idiot.

I mention this because there are many times where someone's Facebook status or blog post has ruffled feathers. It's one thing to disagree, but often people become so irate and you can only assume it is because they have personalized comments that weren't directed at them. Are they feeling judged, or are they judging themselves? I just find it interesting because I don't think people can be offended unless deep inside they think the same thing of themselves. And if someone is judging us, why do we care? I am caring less and less as I get older. I think that is one gift of age. It counterbalances the acts of gravity that are just rude. #mygiveadamnisbusted

June 19

I do try to always look at the silver lining, and for most things I'm able to do that. Seems like when things are really bad or sad, or tragic, I'm able to dig deep and find the lesson. Maybe I do that out of desperation so that I don't find myself plummeting into the pits of hell, complete with moaning and gnashing of teeth. Who knows. But when it comes to the daily grind...and by grind I mean pull your toenails back with a pair of pliers, then shove your head in a meat grinder, kind of grind...I just DO NOT have the capacity. My humor is the only thing that honestly keeps me from running my car into a pole. Yes, it's that bad.

Now don't start with the "Oh Shari, so many people have it

so much worse..." Yeah, yeah, I know all that. That is all completely true. I'll be ashamed of myself later and then add THAT to my list of failures, but for right now I need to wallow. I need to wallow in the madness of my daily life. The constant screeching (think howler monkey), Sissy refusing to eat, while Bubba is eating us out of house and home; the screaming from the tangles in the hair that MAKE ME WANT TO SHAVE HER HEAD, the whining, I could go on and on...and I think I have...so I'm going to stop right here. I know this will pass. And again, this is one of the few thoughts that keeps me going. That it will end and I will never have to do this again. I do not like motherhood right now. There. I said it. So shoot me. (Please!) I wish I could be one of those people who just blows sunshine and rainbow ponies up your butt, but it's just not me.

I think I am missing a gene, the gene that causes some people to need to be needed. I do not need needing, don' t want needing... although I wouldn't mind some kneading...shoulders are kinda tight, but I digress. Some mothers love this feeling, of being needed. Some love it so much that when the young'uns get to be self-sufficient they crave another baby. (Kinda like people who always want puppies but seem to forget that they grow up!) When Sissy says, "I can do it, Mama. I don't need help," my heart soars. Could it be the constant, never-ending fatigue that makes me want to jump up and slap my granny, you ask? Possibly. Or it could be the non-stop feeling of being pecked to death by a chicken, the hanging on my shirt, wrapped around my leg, screeching, pulling at my hair, and slapping at my face (that would be the baby) that makes me long for my children's independence? Probably. Cold hearted? Never. I love them deeply and completely, but please stop touching me. #longstobeahermit

June 30

Goodnight moon! Tonight is the night I shall sleepeth with earplugs. Alas, dear children, I shall not hear your cries. For tonight Mommy sleeps and your father shall watcheth over thee and bitcheth accordingly. Waging the slings and arrows of parenthood, he shall gain perspective and it shall enable him to leave for work Monday morning with a skip in his step, thanking his own personal God that he was not born a woman.

July 5

MEDIC! Yesterday was Sissy's fifth birthday and so I decided to have something simple. Didn't want to do a big party at the house because it is just too hard to get stuff done around the house with Bubba around because the boy is into EVERYTHING. So I decided we would all go bowling. Bowling is fun. Easy. Away from the house. Everyone in the family can participate and have a good time. Wellllll, then I thought we should come back to the house for cake. After checking bowling prices, realized that $7.50 per lane was much better than $25 per lane since I needed three. That means we had to bowl before noon. Okay, 10:30 a.m.-12. Perfect! But then that's lunch. Can't have cake before lunch. (is what they tell me. :)) Okay, so pizza. We will have pizza and cake.

Cue the illness. Sick the ENTIRE week before the party. Can't get up off the couch, much less clean and prepare for the non-party outside of the house that has turned into a non-party in the house. So fast forward to the day before the party. You read that right. Day. Before. Party. I now have a list as long as my arm. Got to clean my floors, vacuum the whole house (thanking the Lord for my big

house but AARRRGGHH!!!), dust, make cupcakes and
decorate them in splendid pink, sparkly glory, hang the
decorations, tidy up the backyard in case peeps want to
hang back there, yadda yadda.

The morning of the party, up at 6:30 a.m. to get ready
before the kidlets are up, get breakfast made, dress kids, at
make it to the bowling alley by 10:30 a.m., whew! Don't
forget the snacks for the baby! Diapers, wipes...what
else?...Sippy!

So, fun was had by all...except the baby...and me...
probably hubby, my mom...pretty much anyone who had
to deal with the baby at all! He was miserable and whiney
and screamy and generally a PITA. (Pain In The Ass.
Please try to keep up, would ya?) But the birthday girl had
fun, we came back to the house and the pizza was
delivered on schedule, cupcakes were yummy and Sissy
never stopped smiling. I told her that today she was five
and she said, "Whaaaat? It's my birthday AND I'm five?!"
:)

So today I'm screaming 'MEDIC!', but totally worth it.
And my story is no different than the millions of moms

around the world who stress and stress, not because we want to make the party perfect in the eyes of others, but to make sure that we create a memorable birthday for out little rugrats who make us wonder what the heck we ever did with all that free time pre-Mommy. #isquanderedmyfreetimeandnowiambeingpunished

July 12

Death to the highchair! Seriously, I'm over it. That flippin' thing has been in my face since November 2005. Mind you, my first child wasn't born until the end of Feb. 2006. And babies don't sit in highchairs until they are at least six months old...which would be August...of 2006!

Right about now you are asking yourself, "Why would the highchair be set up in November BEFORE the baby was born?" To which I would reply, "WHAT'S YOUR POINT?!" It's because I'm an over anxious pain in the ass, that's why! It was our first baby gift and it arrived on the doorstep in November. So of course, being who I am, I sat my pregnant butt down on the floor and put the damn thing together IMMEDIATELY! Not realizing it was the size of my first car...and my apartment was not much bigger than my first car. Not realizing you can't take these mothers apart once they are put together! Don't get me wrong, it is a beautiful highchair. It was the chosen ONE. The highchair that was to fulfill all of my highchair dreams. The one that was so perfect in its perfection that it would inspire my child to crave brussels sprouts and organic legumes. You know, THAT highchair.

So here we are, five and a half years, 5,682 meals later and I want to light the mother effer on FIRE! But realistically, I probably have at least six months left. I will have to suck it up. I think I can...I think I can...and then I'm gonna beat it...I'm gonna pound it with a mallet...except I don't have a mallet. I will go BUY a mallet, THEN I will pound it within an inch of its life! I shall put on my big boots and kick the crap out of it...and it will be glorious. Just thinking about it gives me the warm fuzzies. :) #babycrapbegone

July 30

Today was picture day. Yearly picture day. Bubba is two. I could probably end this story here because if you have children, you know this story is not a happy one. But I can feel that you really want me to share, so I will. Maybe it will be cathartic for me. Maybe it will purge the pain from my body. Or maybe I will be returned to that day in my mind and slam my head through a plate glass window. We'll see. Should be fun.

Now let me be clear, this day was made much worse by the fact that I am not the picture person in the family, meaning the one who gives a crap about the pictures. That would be hubby. It could be said that I am not the picture person because I am the one who has to haul these children to have their picture taken! If he had to take them, he might discover that he isn't the picture person that he thinks he is! Not that I don't enjoy pics of my kids, but as any mother can tell you, we see these captured moments of our children with their upturned cherub-like faces and all we can think is, "Boy, he was a shit that day!", or "Right after this was taken, I put her on eBay." It takes years to forget the trauma and nausea that often accompanies 'picture day.' It must take more than four years because Sissy is five and the experience of her one year photo shoot is still embedded in my mind. I tell myself that it fades with time. I have no proof of this. It's just what I tell myself to get through, but I see it all so clearly. Where's Alzheimer's when ya need it?

Being the non-picture-person that I am, and the fact that I
am absolutely DREADING this day, I haven't purchased
special clothes for the kids. Probably out of denial that
this day is coming or maybe because I refuse to pay any
more money for outfits that they will wear for 10 minutes.
(10 minutes because I am a 'Shock and Awe' type of
mother. But more on that later.) So I find myself on
picture morning digging through their closets and drawers
to find two outfits that look decent together. I do. I rock.
Cue the angels. Now on to hair and makeup. (No makeup
but I enjoy the ring to it.) It isn't until this moment that I
realize it is like Cowlickapalooza up in here! Good LORD!
Not enough gel in the world to deal with all of this. I comb
this way and that way, spike, and consider a razor, before
just leaving it in God's hands. If he wants my boy to look
like chicken, so be it. Actually, that isn't too far off. So on
to the studio. A 20 minute drive. Oh joy.

Now about the Shock and Awe, I have a speech that I give
to all who photograph my kids. "I am going to put this
child down. The minute this tush hits the chair, you start
clicking. I mean you click like you have never clicked
before. Click like you are on FIRE, MAN! Because once
the screaming begins, there's no turning back. There is no

'calm down and go back to pictures in a few minutes.' This is as good as it is going to get and if my children are going to get out of here without a beating, I need to remove them from the area when the screaming commences." By the look on the photog's face, I become Psychic Sue and can deduce whether or not they have children. Bubba was better than Sissy at two in the attitude dept. but worse in the 'can't sit still' dept. He was crawling out of my arms to get onto the picture platform, but after about three and a half seconds there, couldn't wait to get down. And then the lady tried to POSE HIM! HAVE YOU HEARD NOTHING THAT I HAVE SAID?! DOES 'SHOCK AND AWE' RING A BELL? I believe I blurted, "NO POSING! CLICK, WOMAN!" Those of you that know me, know that I would say something like this. It's kind of like Outspoken Tourette's. It runs in the family. Not my fault. :) But it seems to get the job done. I follow it up with a funny little ditty, when time allows.

I think the pictures took all of six minutes, including pics of Bubba alone and some with the two kids. I wish this thing had audio because you just can't translate the sheer VOLUME through the written word. So we had pushing, wriggling, screaming and photos, oh my. The only way we got through the choosing of the pictures portion of the program was thanks to candy. Candy chock full of artificial colors and flavors that ended up all over the picture clothes and me. But hey, at least I didn't end up with poop on my face. That seems to be the benchmark of bad days for me. What's that you say? You don't know this story? Well, that is due in part to the post-traumatic stress disorder that the 'Poop Incident of 2009' inflicted on me. I have tried to write this story on several occasions but can only get through bits and pieces at a time. Someday I will finish it. Probably as the book is going to print. I mean, I shared the pee story, why not tell #2. Literally. ;)

So pics are done for another year. HALLELUJAH! Got some cute ones, or maybe they are just cute to me because they are done. Neither here nor there. All that matters is that next year Bubba will be three and he HAS to be easier, right? Right?! If you aren't agreeing, you must leave. Mommy can't look at you right now.

Poop,
There it Is!

August 4

Okay, "Poop" here it is. The story that has never been put into print, but has been requested more than any other by those who have been witness to the full throttle, animated real-life version. ~Deep breath~ While this story is funny to many, and I can understand why, it is one of those stories that a parent will laugh at AS LONG AS YOU weren't the parent that it happened to. In fact, it seems to kick the hilarity up a few notches by the fact that it happened to someone else. I can appreciate the humor. It is funny. I have yet to laugh about it, but I am sure someday I will. Not now. I'm still healing. Two years later and it is as...uh...*fresh (yuck)*...as it was the day it happened.

I should warn you that if you have a weak stomach, you might want to look away. If you don't have children, it may become necessary to avert your eyes. Once you have kids you will find that poop just becomes a natural part of everyday conversation, much like discussing that pumpkin lattes are back at Starbucks. Let me give you an example,

"Hey, did you see that Starbucks has pumpkin lattes again?"

"Wow, great! Hey, Sissy pooped on the floor today. It was kind of yellow."

"Weird. Wanna order pizza?"

"Sure."

Something like that.

Okay, so I'm stalling. I really never wanted to retell this

story. It was pretty traumatic for me. But you see, I have
friends who don't seem to give a shit (pardon the pun),
and insist that it must be logged (again, pardon) for
posterity.

So once upon a time, Sissy was three and I decided to potty
train. Knowing her personality, I decided to wait until she
was three because I wanted to make sure she was really
ready. With a new baby on the horizon, I decided to give it
a go.

Day two and things seemed to be chugging along
UNTILLLLLL she pooped in her panties. I remember
EXACTLY where she was standing. It's as if that moment
is frozen in my memory because on some level I knew I
was entering the gates of hell. Sissy was standing on the
landing of the staircase *screaming* like no human being
I've ever heard. No big whoop, I'm thinking. I went and
changed her, easy peasy. HA! Little did I know that a
series of events had begun in her little mind. She decided
that she would never poop again. Ever. Never. No poop
for her! Even when I put her back into Pull-Ups almost
immediately, promising she never had to wear panties
again all the days of her life. Mama would wipe her butt

forever and ever, amen. But no, the poop strike continued and this led to the constant crying and screaming, "My bottom hurts! My bottom hurts!" non-stop all day. All day. (Just for giggles, record your kid screaming the same thing over and over and then I want you to play that on repeat for three months. Yes, you read that right. THREE MONTHS. Of screaming that her bottom hurts.) I thought I was honestly going to go INSAAAAAAANE. "I know your bottom hurts. You need to poop. You will feel better! I promise!" It fell on deaf ears. I couldn't give her a bath without her screaming because the water relaxed her and it made it more difficult to hold it, but hold it she did! My girl is nothing if not stubborn and extremely strong! IronButt be thy name.

After several days of her refusing to poop, suppositories, and mama LITERALLY holding her in a crouching position to try to force it out (TMI, I know! I called this pose Crouching Mama, Pooping Dragon.) I called the doctor. The nurse heard her screaming in the background and interrupted me by saying, "Honey, are you home alone?"...uh, yeah..."I need you to hang up the phone and get her to the emergency room"...okay..."Something has to be done. She will be fine, but you can't live this way!"

THANK YOU!!!!! Off to the emergency room we go! I had to call hubby on the way and have him meet us there because if they needed to x-ray her, I wouldn't be able to go in because I was pregnant and couldn't be around the radiation. Let's have a little sidebar here while I paint the picture...you've all been to the emergency room before, so I want you to visualize that. Now picture a three-year-old screaming like she is on fire. Nonstop. The whole time you are there. So that is like, what? Three hours minimum? We are sitting on a bed with the little curtain pulled around us. I am sure that is helping muffle the banshee-like screams. ~rolls eyes~ As the doctors finally come over to take Sissy and hubby to the x-ray lab, they leave a gap in the curtain. I am sitting my big ole self on the bed, crying. As I look up I see my good friend standing there looking at me, also crying. Her grandma was taken to the emergency room and they were a few beds over. She says, "That was *Sissy* screaming?! Because we were ready to give that kid our spot in line just to make her stop!" Apparently, they were cursing the screaming child (me, too!) and praying someone would sedate her! Who could blame them when it was going on for hours?! It had actually been going on for longer than that, just not in public. Only for her mother to hear. Lucky me.

Motherhood is such a blessing. It is a calling. Too bad I didn't answer the calling for Fatherhood. THAT is the gig you want! But I digress.

So doctors do an x-ray, enema (which is a whole other Oprah that hubby should tell himself. I recall the term "ShitStorm2009" being mentioned a few times. Finally, one story that didn't involve me directly!) Doctors said she was all cleaned out and needed to see a pediatric specialist to decide what the problem was and how to proceed. Very scary for any parent to hear that your child needs to go to a specialist. So fast-forward to specialist saying we need more blood tests to decide if the problem is physical or behavioral. Off to the hospital again to have blood taken.

I am holding Sissy in my lap with her blankie, Mother Nurse is on one side and Non-Mother Nurse is on the other. You will understand in a minute why I have named them accordingly without them having to tell me whether or not they have children. Mother Nurse says to hug Sissy tightly and hold one arm down, while she holds the 'arm of interest'. Non-Mother Nurse shall do the sticking. As we are all chatting about how worried I am, praying there isn't something physically wrong with her, ooooh what a scary situation this is, so worried...so much worry...and thennnnnn enter the needle. THE SECOND that needle hit Sissy's arm I lost all hearing in my left ear (from the scream) and felt a warm whoooooosh upon my legs. :l Followed by the smell of a truck stop restroom after the boys have had the chili con carne special. In my shock, all I could say was, "Well, it's not physical!"

Here's how I knew their motherhood status...Mother Nurse started laughing and Non-Mother Nurse turned white as a ghost and ran from the room. Last I heard she was still in therapy and had her vagina sewn shut. But back to me...I stood up as quickly as I could and flung Blankie over my shoulder to save it from a fate worse than death. (This entire time Sissy is screaming and kicking. SHOCKER!) As Blankie goes over my shoulder I feel this *SMAAAAAACK* across my cheek. There was no mistaking what had just happened, and if I had ANY doubt, I only had to look at Mother Nurse for confirmation. "Whoops. I'll get wipes," she says. Thanks.

Have you ever tried to clean up diarrhea coming from a flailing child who has been on adult doses of Miralax for a week, while trying to lay them on an exam table with that

MADDENING paper that disintegrates at the slightest drop of liquid and then proceeds to stick to everything it touches?!!!! No? I HAVE!!!! It was like wrestling a ferret. Or maybe an octopus with ferret-like tendencies. Either way, it was loud, smelly, sticky, CRAZY! I just wanted to die. I was covered in shit and so was she. At least she had an excuse, she was three. I was just a pitiful six-month pregnant mother of a toddler with a nervous disorder and dark circles.

Sidebar...it is at this moment in our story, ladies and gentlemen, that I realized we are discussing poop. I apologize. It's gross. This will be the segment that separates the men from the boys...or the parents from those with a life. Now back to our regularly scheduled program...

We finally had to wrap Sissy up in a blanket to hold her down and get the blood drawn. Like we really needed the blood at this point? Mystery SOLVED, people! She is just stubborn and don't wanna! AAAGGGHHH!!! So results come back and ...hold on to your hats...it's BEHAVIORAL! Thank you, doctor. He said that was the good news *and* the bad news. We were going to have to ride this one out until she matured enough to decide to poop. In the meantime, she was on adult doses of Miralax for the next several months. We could never really leave the house because I never knew when she would...um...unleash, so to speak. And when that happened it was traumatizing in itself. Just the sheer VOLUME was unbelievable, much more than a Pull-Up could handle. The BEST part about all of that is that we had our condo on the market and sometimes, after holding it in for seven days, she would let it all go on our new beige carpet. This often happened as the realtor was calling saying she was around the corner with prospective buyers. They were excited! I was excited too, but for all the wrong reasons. I was scrambling to open windows, light candles, clean the carpet, wash the clothes and bathe Sissy, all in less than 30 minutes. Who says that being a SAHM doesn't prepare you for handling ANY crisis that life throws at you? I never learned anything close to this in my corporate life! Nothing kills a house sale like the smell of shit. Amen.

So how did it all end? (So to speak! Ba-dum-bum! Thankyouverymuch, I'll be here all weekend. :)) Well, Hubby got me tickets to go to Chicago and see Oprah and I was NOT going to miss that! I worried about leaving him home with Sissy for three days so I got some homeopathic 'calming' tablets for her to take while I was gone. I called when I got to Chicago because I was so worried and really feeling guilty for leaving at such a hard time. So here is me, "Hi honey, how are things?"...hubby, "GREAT! We had a wonderful day so far! I gave her some of the calming tablets and a little while later she told me she had to poop so I put her on the potty and she did it! No muss, no fuss!" ARE YOU EFFING KIDDING ME?!!!! I wanted to kick him in the balls. I can't lie. Of course I was happy she was doing better but COME ON! Isn't that just the way it always goes? Daddy swoops in and gets the glory. Every. Freakin'. Time! Blood, sweat, and shit for the moms, but daddy gets to be the hero! Whatever! At least I have Oprah. Maybe it will be her Favorite Things Show! Dare I dream? Alas, THAT was not meant to be. I got to sit and bawl my eyes out for an hour listening to stories about child porn. No gifts under *my* seat! All I got was a box of Kleenex and a lifetime of nightmares.

So the moral of the story is...I have no clue. There is no moral sometimes and life just sucks. How's that? Then it shits all over you and you have to take it, clean it up and try to get it to stop screaming! And maybe make lemonade, or something like that. THIS is the kind of conversation that needs to be happening in health classes in high schools across America! If that won't scare them into abstinence, nothing will. Maybe that is my next calling, high school health teacher! Sit down class, Mrs. Brown has a few stories to tell. Be afraid, be very afraid. :) #ifyoucantstandtheshitstayoutofthebedroom

August 8

I have given birth to Howard Cosell. If you don't know who that is, please pretend you do or I fear I shall never recover from the realization that I am getting old. Middle aged, even. ~heavy sigh~ But I digress, having birthed Howard definitely has its advantages. If it wasn't for her every ninety second account of Bubba's doings, I wouldn't be able to run upstairs to grab the laundry. Howard makes sure I know exactly what her little brother is doing every flingin' flangin' second of every day...which is fun. So is a sharp stick in the eye. Good times.

August 12

Here's a peeve...people who ask and answer their own

questions! Why do they do it? We don't know. Is it annoying? Yes it is. Are they incapable of formulating a statement? Probably. Makes them feel important? I guess so. I hear it all the time and it makes. Me. Crazy. :$

Let's take Carmaggedon, for example...wait, what?...you don't know what CARMAGGEDON is? You mean to tell me that the entire universe isn't waiting, holding their breath, to see what happens this weekend when they close a ten mile stretch of the 405 freeway in Los Angeles for 53 hours? SAY IT ISN'T SO! (I kid.) Is Carmaggedon going to be the biggest shit storm L.A. has ever seen? Yes. Will most people stay home like they are told? No. Will the news give us bumper-to-bumper coverage 24/7 and come up with names even MORE ridiculous than Carmaggedon? Yes. Can we expect phrases like TrafficWatch 2011? Parking-lot-apolis? Unfortunately, yes. Are you getting my point? I hope so.

If you have something to say, SAY it. Don't ask it and then cut me off to answer it! Wastes precious time that nobody has and just lets the cat out of the bag that you are a pretentious ASS. :) #doyouloveme #ithinkyoudo

August 20

Bathroom music and ventilation. Seems like a natural
combination to me. Then tell me WHY, when I am at the
mall...a restaurant...the store...I walk into the bathroom
~screeching of tires~ and it is stuffy and *silent*. No air. No
noise. Except those lovely nature sounds. Oh, and of
course Howard is there announcing to the entire room,
"You gotta go pee, Mommy? Poopies too, or just pee-pees?
WOW! That's a lot of pee pees! Good job, Mommy!"
Thank you, Howard. Of all the places that NEED music
and ventilation, I would say the bathroom ranks right up
there! Am I wrong? I don't think so. Is it a conspiracy?
Possibly. Who in their right mind wouldn't ventilate the
BATHROOM?! It boggles my mind. Could it be THAT
much more expensive? I don't think so. Is it worth it? Yes.
Yes it is.

Here's a fun story: I was traveling on business back in
1996. A co-worker and I were in the ladies room at the
airport and I commented about how it was too quiet in
there. Why wasn't there ever any music in the ladies'
room?! At that exact moment we heard someone fart and
without skipping a beat my girlfriend says, "Well there ya

go!" :) Doesn't GET any funnier than that!

Even way back then I was ranting about this subject. I can't be the only one who has noticed this travesty! It has been a bee in my bonnet for about fifteen years! #ihaveahardtimelettingthingsgo.

August 24

Question. How many half grains does it take to make a whole? I'm trying to justify my dinner. And shouldn't coffee be considered a vegetable since it comes from a plant? Or maybe a protein because it is a bean? Legume? What is a legume, really? I have no clue but it makes me feel fancy and healthy to say legume. Legume...legume. The word's lost all meaning.

Okay, so we've got half grains (I think in France it is pronounced le' donut), we've got coffee, some skim milk since I am all about health, and vanilla which must also be a vegetable because I've seen the pods...or are they beans? BEANS! More protein! I am awesome. #donthatetheplayahatethegame

August 27

Howard Cosell has now become Howard the Translator.
Baby Bubba talks nonstop. Non. Stop. As in, never stops
talking. In case you didn't get that...he talks a lot. So now
not only do I hear, "Mommy, tika tika blah blah cookie,
monkey george, outside, water, ickies, milk, go bye bye,
Abby, Sissy" times a bazillion, but it is always followed by
Howard's translations: "Mom, he said he wants a salami
sandwich at Disneyland," "Mom, he said he wants to go to
Target and get a water balloon made of cheese. Oh, and a
ICEE." You know when you watch the U.N. (cuz you know
you do) and the translator starts talking before the foreign
dude is even finished? Yeah, it's like that.

Funerals Can be Fun

September 1

Motherhood is similar to being an air traffic controller. There's incoming, outgoing, and potential life threatening disasters. It is hectic, there's lots of talking, and it requires complete and total focus. You don't get much sleep. Copious amounts of coffee are involved. You find yourself shouting orders and directing traffic while doing a million other things, and the trick is for each child to realize when you are talking to THEM.

Sure, you could call out each of their names before a

sentence, but at some point the names all run together and when you are trying to get pertinent, often life-saving information out in a jiffy, there isn't always time. Besides, odds are you will say the wrong name first which will then confuse the whole lot of them and it will take longer to explain that you made a mistake and clarify WHO you are speaking to than to just point and shoot.

You see, it will start out all nice and civilized like this... "Bubba, stop wiggling. You're going to fall off the changing table. Hold still! I'm almost done. Sissy, DO NOT throw your Barbies over the railing. You could hit someone on the head! STOP WIGGLING! No, not you, I'm talking to your brother! I will NOT go get that Barbie. You threw it, you go get it. Not YOU! YOU stay still! Not YOU! I am serious, you are gonna go to bed if you don't knock it off. Stop crying, I'm not talking to you! ENOUGH! Do you want to go to bed? NOT. TALKING. TO. YOU! That's it! Everyone get in bed!!!" ~cue scary mommy growl as my eyes roll back in my head~ "NOWWWWWWW!"

We were recently at the pool and both kids were standing in front of me, clad with their life jackets and ready to go.

I was in the pool and I kid you not, complete with hand motions I found myself saying, "Okay, come to mom, baby. Move out of sister's way. Don't push him! Watch your head on the rail. Let her get by. Move over here. Don't touch the bee! I gotcha. Let go of her hair. He didn't mean it. He's a baby. You're okay. Go over there. NO TOUCHING BEE! Now he wants out. No. You're staying in. We just got here. No, you don't have to get out. No 'bye-bye'. Stop crying, we aren't going home! You aren't running all over like a wild man. We ARE 'bye-bye'! The water is not that cold. It's a hot day. I think we will survive..." and then you pull out the big guns...you go where you swore you'd never go..."DO YOU HAVE ANY IDEA what I would have given to have my mom take me to the pool when I was a kid?! DO YOU!?" As I glance over I see two twenty-somethings staring at me with their mouths hanging open. All I could muster was, "Oh yeah, it's a party."

After thirty minutes of this non-stop joy, I throw (not literally, but almost) these children into the wagon because we are gonna GET THE HELLLLL out of there! As my crazy-ass self is hauling them away, I can't help but dole out some useful advice to these mere fetuses lounging in the pool..."Don't have kids! Stick with dogs. It sucks! SUCKS, SUCKS, SUCKS! And just when you think the sucking is over...it's gonna suck even more. More and more sucking until you die. And then that sucks, too! Amen." I'll be the first to admit, it was a rough day. They thought I was kidding and they laughed. What do you want to bet that at some point in the future they will be in a similar sitch and remember that 'crazy-ass woman at the pool'? Consider yourself warned. Oh...did I mention I love my kids? ;) #wheresmyhazardpay

September 4

I needed a sympathy card. Sympathy cards are tough because it has to be just right. Not too religious, if they aren't the religious type. Not too overly familiar, if it was just an acquaintance. So the search was on...'sorry for your loss', 'there are no words', 'my heart goes out to you', 'enjoy the heat'...~SCREEEEEEEEEEEECHING tires~ WHAT THE?!!!! ~blink, blink~ Oooohhhhh!!! I had apparently drifted into the Bon Voyage section. ~cue uncontrollable-afraid-I'm-gonna-pee-my-pants laughter~ So now I can't stop. I keep looking at bon voyage cards with death in mind. Never have I had more fun. Phrases like ...'have a nice trip'...'you deserve it'...'wish I could be there'...'bring sunscreen', had me looking like an idiot. I was almost doubled over in hysterics, with tears streaming down my face and from all appearances, I was perusing the sympathy section. Some probably thought I was overcome by grief, others may have thought I had a complete psychotic break. Maybe it was a little bit of both. Might I suggest to Mr. Card Man that he move the Bon Voyage section? Next time you need a pick-me-up, do yourself a favor and try this. I highly recommend it.

September 7

I'm going to videotape a message to my future self. I am going to tell my future self not to get too upset when my teenagers lock themselves in their rooms and never come out. I will say, "ENJOY IT! Remember this?"...and then I'll cut to a video of these screaming banshees running through the house as I beg them to keep it down to fog-horn level! Pictures of distorted faces because they are SO CLOSE that the camera can't figure out what the hell to focus on! I have many friends with teenagers, and I also remember being a teenager locked in my room all day and how it drove my mother crazy. I am sure that when the time comes I will have similar feelings, but at this moment, I have a hard time imagining such a thing. Especially now that my littlest angel is talking and saying "Mommy!" 6,342 times a day at full volume.

I'd like to think of myself as an Advocate for Independence! If you feel like you need to keep your little self locked up all day, GOOD FOR YOU! I'm here in full support! Depending on your age, I might be at the mall in full support...or maybe at a movie in full support...lunch?... who knows! But sweet potato, wherever I am, and whatever lovely beverage I am sipping on, just know that Mama supports your independence! I shall dine al fresco and salute you! #thisiswhyGodmademargaritas

September 10

So, my grandma died. My sweet little, roly-poly, smells-like-grape-candy grandma. She actually did smell like grape candy. I never quite realized what the smell was until she passed away and I got her recipes. I put them away in a plastic bag and when I opened it a few days later to look through them, it smelled just like her. That's when I realized...grape candy! She was the best grandma ever and we were all devastated to lose our little Gomma. (That's what we called her.)

She only wanted a graveside service because she didn't like all the fuss. So there we were, all of her family and friends, grieving deeply. I almost couldn't breathe that day, the pain was so heavy. Enter...Aunt Ellen. Dear, sweet, very Southern Aunt Ellen. She was Gomma's eldest sister. The two talked on the phone every day at four o'clock. Aunt Ellen still lived in Arkansas where they were both raised, while Gomma lived in California. Aunt Ellen was ninety-one so she couldn't make the trip to Gomma's service. My cousin decided to call her as the preacher began and put her on speakerphone so she could listen. Aunt Ellen was so happy, and we were too. What a great idea. So nice she could participate in some way from such a long distance. At that moment we had no idea the level of participation we were about to enjoy.

Now, I probably don't have to tell you that at ninety-one, Aunt Ellen wasn't up on the latest technology. She didn't understand that when one is on speakerphone, not only can one hear...but one can also be HEARD. I think you know where I'm going with this story. Thinking back, I can see where my Howard Cosell gets it. Must run in the family, this play-by-play commentary.

So the service started with a lovely song from my cousin. As she is singing, I heard Aunt Ellen in her heavy Southern drawl, "Oh baybee! You're doing a great job, bayyyybeee! Auntie is so proud of you bayyybeee!" We couldn't help but giggle, and yet it wasn't until the preacher started the service that it became crystal clear that Aunt Ellen had no idea we could hear HER. We could ALL hear her. It went something like this...

"We are gathered here today to celebrate the life of Sally Temple." (Aunt Ellen: "Yes we are bayyybeee!") The preacher jerked his head up to see where the voice was coming from. Not sure he knew at that moment that he was being heckled by a ninety-one- year-old woman on speakerphone. We all looked at each other like, "Oh shit. Here we go."

"Sally was such a loving woman ("Yes she was, honey!") who was loved by so many. ("We loved her so much, bayyybee.") She also loved the Lord. ("Yes she did, bayyybee! She loved you, Jesus!") This continued for about fifteen minutes with Aunt Ellen shouting out encouragements to the preacher such as "you're doing a great job, bayybee!" at regular intervals. My personal favorite was when the preacher had been going on for a bit and clear as a bell we all heard her say, "Well that preacher sure is a long-winded fella, isn't he?" Stopped the preacher in his tracks. The poor little guy just stopped and stared at us. It was like a cartoon where you could hear him blink. I wanted to crawl under the chair and burrow my way back home. But he was a trooper and continued on, to Aunt Ellen's dismay.

Another cousin got up to say a few words and he mentioned how he had stepped away from the family for a time to which Aunt Ellen responded, "We know ya did, bayybee! We didn't know why but we love ya and are glad you're back!" As I got up to tell a few stories about what a great grandma she was, and how much we loved her, I got the honor of a few comments myself. "She loved you too, bayyybeee!" I couldn't help it, I had to respond, "Thank you, Aunt Ellen." She said, "Oh you're welcome, bayybee. Love you!" Never in my life have I had such a good time at a funeral. My sister and I were laughing so hard that we were shaking. People in the rows behind us thought we were crying. Technically, we were. I definitely had tears streaming down my face.

My first thought was that Aunt Ellen's interjections were going to ruin the service. I soon saw it as a gift. I'd like to think my grandma was smiling down on us and enjoying the fact that we had laughter and joy at her funeral. How many people can say that? Not many, I'd imagine. I look back on that funeral with such fondness and will never forget it as long as I live. Honestly one of the funniest moments of my life.

Aunt Ellen died a few years later, but I couldn't find anyone who would hold the phone up for me. They don't know what they were missin'! #longingtoheckleafuneral

September 13

Not sure I could have been a stay-at-home mom back when my mom raised us. In fact, I know I couldn't. How did they survive the midnight minutiae without a DVR? Episodes of *Oprah*, *Desperate Housewives*, The Real Housewives of Who Cares, all kept me company when I felt like the entire world was sleeping except for me. I felt like a bat...or maybe a vampire. Like I had a whole other existence in the dark of night.

In the morning, when the rest of the world woke up and was out and about, they had no idea all I had accomplished in the last eight hours. Or why I had no sympathy when they said they were tired. Call the waaaaaambulance and shut the hell up!

Can you imagine not even having a VCR? Remember when the TV stations stopped airing programs after 1 a.m.? PERISH THE THOUGHT!!! At least give me an infomercial so I can LEARN something! So I can find out what is missing in my life and wonder how I never realized it before that very moment!

I will tell you what REALLY saved me: My iPad! My little buddy. It literally saved me and gave me an attitude adjustment! As I chased the kids from room to room I could sit on the floor while they played and I could read, play games, Facebook, watch videos, email, whatever! I think it helped keep my brain from turning to complete mush. Instead of handing out free diaper bags at the hospitals, they need to hand out iPads to every mother.

"Here, you're gonna need this." Wouldn't that be fantastic?! Post-partum depression be gone! #YOUgetanipadYOUgetanipad

September 16

I have two strange sights in my neighborhood. One is a woman who pushes her dog around in a stroller. Not a baby stroller, a special dog stroller. Looks like a baby stroller, only smaller and more ridiculous. I don't see any casts or "wheel legs" on the back of that dog to signify an injury which would require such wheeling around. I just don't get it. Aren't dogs supposed to walk? Don't they LIKE to walk? Maybe he has a heart condition. Although if my dog had a heart condition that required me to push him around in a stroller, I'd have to have yellow caution tape and several big ass signs that stated that "DUE TO A HEART CONDITION, I AM REQUIRED TO PUSH MY DOG AROUND IN THIS STUPID STROLLER." The dog seems to want out. I would too if I lived with a crazy woman who pushed me around in a stroller and acted like I was a baby. It's called Gepetto Syndrome, lady. Look into it.

Now the second strangest sight is a lady who jogs every day, all day. That isn't the strangest part. She is a very small woman...with very large...um...accoutrements...or implants, if you will. Not lip implants, or a chin implant, although if she did have either of those implants you wouldn't notice because you couldn't get past the other implants. She has a pair of them and I will leave it at that. She insists on jogging in the tiniest outfits you have ever seen. And pearls. Mustn't forget the pearls. Her tan is like this...have you ever seen the movie, *There's Something About Mary?* You know the old woman with the tan? It's like that. If you haven't seen the movie...then you get out less than I do! Picture a leather bomber jacket and you've got an idea. She has the blondest hair that is in a ponytail on top of her head, circa 1987. There may even be a scrunchie trapped in there somewhere. Speaking of 1987, she may be wearing slouchy socks and high-top Reeboks, now that you mention it. I just want to moisturize that woman head-to-toe, every time I see her! That hair, that skin! Heavens! I'd call *Extreme Makeover* to help but I don't know if they'd be able to catch her.

#Ty'srunningwithabullhorn

September 19

I don't know why I'm so surprised that motherhood doesn't give me a constant thrill. I gave myself some new perspective while having dinner with a good friend the other night. She was talking about how cute my kids were and how much they have grown. I agreed, yes they were cute. God made them that way as a survival mechanism. It is often what keeps us from eating our young. She laughed but I really wanted her to understand the other side of the cute coin. I really wanted her to GET the feeling of being a stay-at-home mom and doing NOTHING ELSE but caring for these children 24/7. Especially after her comment that she wanted my life.

No, I said, you want kids but you don't want my life. Not as it is right now. Not the 24/7-ness of it all. Maybe a few hours here and there might be nice. But when you are responsible for raising polite, respectful, well-adjusted, level-headed, adults...yes, I said ADULTS because we are not raising them to be children, we are raising them to be ADULTS, aren't we?! It is a lot of pressure and stress!

So here is the analogy I gave her... (it ain't perfect, but it gets to the heart of the matter.) What if I told you that starting tomorrow morning, you were going to have to get up at 3 a.m. and go work at a home for the elderly for the next six years? You are not going to have any days off, unless you BEG someone, or pay them (which by the way, this gig doesn't pay) to cover your patients. You will be responsible for providing them with EVERYTHING they need because they can't care for themselves. They will be cranky and yell at you often, and will probably cry three to six times a day. They will wake up screaming at all hours of the night. Very rarely will both of them sleep at the same time.

They will ask for a peanut butter and jelly sandwich for lunch, and after you bring it to them, they will react like you just told them they were adopted. They will become offended by this sandwich on what appears to be a cellular level. The reaction will completely blow your mind and make you wonder if you aren't working in a psych ward. You are. You are in a psych ward and nobody knows it, except other mothers. But most of those mothers appear to like it, treasure it, even! They will not stop smiling. You know there's something else underneath that but they just won't crack! What is wrong with me...or you? Okay, I've gotten a bit lost, but you get the point. Welcome to Crazytown and have a nice day.

People will tell you how lucky you are to stay home, not realizing that it isn't luck but sacrifice and rigorous planning and budgeting which allows you to stay home but forbids you from going ANYWHERE ELSE because there is no extra money! Oh sure, you could pretend you were the federal government and take out loan after loan, but then you'd be in trillion dollars of debt with a poor credit rating, and who needs that extra stress?! And somehow, by feeling the need to vent or get a few moments away, this makes you ungrateful and causes people to judge and question your love for your children. I love my parents, but doesn't mean I want to be a caregiver 24/7. Sure the kids are smaller than adults, so it should make them easier. Well, I suppose diaper changes ARE easier, so you've got me there. But the added layer of them being smaller and cuter is that there is more guilt. "How can I feel this way?", "What is wrong with me?", "I'm a horrible person" soon follows.

Well, talk about throwing a turd in the punchbowl! Once I had finished spewing this rant to my friend, she was completely white. I mean, she is white anyway, but she was even WHITER! And I believe her mouth was hanging open like a bass. Not bass the instrument, bass the fish. Big mouthed bass. Mission accomplished. I believe I had finally explained the feeling I have every day. It just feels good when you think somebody 'gets' you. So that is when I smiled, toasted and finished my drink. I was feeling the satisfaction of being understood. She was in a state of shock...or awe...shock and awe...I don't know but she wasn't moving.

It is the story that is not often told. We hear bad stories on the news but it is usually followed by an arrest. The tough, down in the trenches stories of mothers who are good parents but struggle with the level of intensity it requires to be consistent with your kids, not give up and allow them to roll those eyes, get up and walk across that room ONE MORE TIME to get their attention and correct them, those stories are not often told. The right thing is most often the hard thing. And it is so easy and understandable as to why so many parents give up and shrug it off. It is too hard. And those of us who stick to it, end up sounding like horrible people. I guess we don't sound horrible to each other, but to those without kids, or who aren't with them constantly, or who may happen to have been blessed with easy children. (I don't think many children are easy, but I am sure there are a few.) If I had only had Sissy, and not Bubba, I would have thought that people were just lazy when it came to raising kids. That getting them to sleep through the night required just a few days of commitment. Sissy was a very easy baby, and a little challenging as a toddler, but NOTHING like Bubba. He really taught me that one parenting situation is not like another. Every experience is different, just like every person is different. And one child's personality will work great with one parent, and drive the other parent to look for that hidden box of cupcakes in the back of the pantry...or was that wine? Potato, potah-to!

So I tell my story at the risk of being chastised and judged. It's okay, I'm a big girl and I can take it. I can take it because it is my truth. And it is the truth of millions of men and women who do this every day. There is something freeing, which lightens the burden a bit, when others share your situation. Something that makes you feel like you aren't alone and you aren't a horrible person because you cannot stand, FOR ONE MORE SECOND, to hear a child scream or whine. I ended my story by asking my friend to go home and turn on some rap music. Turn it up as loud as it will go! SO loud that you are sure the neighbors will call the cops. Now leave it on for twelve hours. THAT is what it is like. :) (No offense to those who enjoy rap music, I just happen to know that my friend does not.)

So that night I left feeling a little bit lighter, knowing that I had been understood. I slept like a baby, which you all know is a JOKE. Those suckers don't sleep well at all! Okay, so I slept like a fifteen-year-old boy! That's it. And hopefully, my girlfriend slept better having been given a big dose of perspective. #JuneCleaverisabitch

Corn Dogs
are the
Devil

September 21

Well, it is official. I am the mother of a kindergartener! Where has the time gone? I'll tell you exactly where, right down to the month, because this has been a lonnnnng five years! And a lot of hard work has gone into creating this sweet, kind, and bright little thing so that she is ready and able to take on the rigors of kindergarten! I am proud to say she is ready, and Mama and Daddy are for sure ready! Mama is a little more ready than Daddy, I think, since he will be seeing her the same number of hours per week that he always has.

If I allow myself to sit and think of the momentous occasion this is, I could get sentimental and teary-eyed. But then two minutes later she is going to tell me that her "tummy says it doesn't eat dinner anymore," or she's going to get a hangnail and cry about it for two and a half weeks, and I'm right back to my state of readiness.

I prefer to look upon this time with excitement that we've gotten to this point without Child Protective Services getting involved. That we both survived the midnight feedings, learning to walk and talk, potty training (Oy vey, that one liked to have killed me), and two years of preschool.

Five-year-olds carry their own challenge in that the smart mouth is there, the tone is there, but yet they still don't 100% get what they are saying. Case in point, when I tell my daughter to watch her mouth and she replies in earnest that she can't see her mouth. Or when you tell them to stop back-talking and they inform you that they aren't talking to your back, they are talking to your front. I think the attitude is in the bud stages, preparing to fully bloom when they hit thirteen. This is why it is imperative to squash this 'tude before it takes root! I'm not kidding. I know parents who think that their children were angels until they hit thirteen. Hate to tell ya, I knew that kid was an a-hole when he was six!!! He's just bigger now! Poor kid, it isn't his fault he's an a-hole. It is his parents who were either too busy or too lazy to do anything to stop his behavior when it was just in its sapling stage. Consistency is exhausting but necessary. I applaud the parents I see who are on top of their kids and who don't tolerate back-talkers talking to their fronts. #justsayno

September 22

Hiccups. You can't enter The Pantry if you have hiccups. True story. I had the hiccups today. First time since I was twelve. (And as a sidebar...when did I get so old that hiccups now make me tired? They are EXHAUSTING! All of the hiccuping, the jumping, enough already!) I realized as I was jonesing for some pantry time that I could not escape into my quiet haven. It lets the cat out of the bag and defeats the purpose. Part of the beauty o' the pantry is that the children don't know you are in there. If they did, there would be little hands reaching under the door for you, pounding on your beloved pantry door. It just wouldn't work. So on to Plan B...cookies.

September 25

I miss cooking...

I know, I know, don't hate me! But I do. It hit me yesterday that part of my frustration with little Bubba is that I don't have the time to cook or plan out my meals like I used to. I feel like I throw stuff together last minute. It's still healthy, but just not fun for me. It has gotten to where I have lost the desire to even try because I know that every 3 1/2 minutes I will be interrupted to go get this, wipe that, break up a fight, fix Buzz's wing or dislodge a pony from some place where it shouldn't oughtta be. I guess, in essence, I have cried 'uncle'.

My girlfriends know me, I can become obsessed with a cookbook and recipes and go on cooking binges for days talking of nothing but soup! Hypothetically speaking, of course. ;) Okay, so there's a story there but I'll save that for another day. But all this baby business has just been cramping my style for a long time now (love you Bubba, just being honest), add in the pregnancy from hell and I just miss doing the stuff that makes me, ME!
When we moved into our beautiful house we had the

kitchen completely remodeled (this was at the exact same time that I had the baby...did I mention that? ;)) and it is beautiful! Definitely a cook's kitchen complete with a six burner cooktop, double oven, tons of counter space and an island. Add to that, all of my beautiful pots and pans, my tools and gadgets, my dish obsession, and cake stand obsession, and mug obsession, and cookie jar obsession... OK! OK! WHAT'S YOUR POINT?! Well, it is just sad that I can't take more advantage of it, that's all. I have dreams of Sunday dinners. I remember when I used to cook all day on Sundays and I loved it! Trying out new recipes, and filling the house with amazing smells. Aaaaahhhh... someday. It won't always be this way, right? RIGHT?!!!! Please tell me that all of my 'Martha Stewart Christmases' won't go to waste! (This is how my family referred to the years when there was nothing but kitchen stuff on my list.) I refer to them as the wonder years. Good times.

So just a little venting for today...maybe tomorrow, too. Having a rough time of it in Mommyland lately and needing something to get me back in touch with myself and relieve some of this stress. It seems like at the end of the day I'm desperately trying to find something to take this feeling away. This feeling like I can't catch my breath.

(I had it so badly the other day and then realized I was actually having an asthma episode. I literally couldn't breathe.) Have you ever felt like you were crawling out of your skin? And I just want to scream, or run, or run screaming...until it goes away. I usually get it to go away right before I go to bed so I can get up and do it all over again. Some days it is a walk or a run, some days a glass of wine. I'm trying to stay away from cake. Cake would be bad. It would be sooooo good, but then it would be bad.

Okay, this has gotten way too heavy and I've gone to the dark, twisty place. Someone's screaming, and it isn't me this time (I checked), so that's my cue. Muah!

September 28

I am putting this house on a crumb-free diet! There's gluten-free, peanut-free, carb-free, and now crumb-free. Because I swear to all that is holy, that I cannot take one more day of crumbs on the floor, crumbs in the carpet, stuck to the bottom of my foot, all over everyone and every thing that isn't nailed down. Well actually, there are crumbs on those things, too. If we had a dog I'd name him Crumb Head because that is exactly what he'd look like!

And correct me if I am wrong, but granola bar crumbs are the WORST!!! Stepping on those sons-a-bitches with or without socks makes. Me. CR@ZY!!!!!!!!!!!!

So, I am in the works to develop a diet for my children...a meal plan, if you will...that eliminates any and all things that can create a crumb! I shall call it The Crumb Free Diet and it shall be huge. Mothers from all over the world shall read this diet and nod in agreement saying, "Yes, dear friend. Yesssssssss!" They shall salute me in public for my vision. They shall do the slow, loud clap at the airport as I disembark. I shall be the leader of the Crumb Free Nation and wield my power with kindness and foresight. For this world is in need of less crumbs, and mothers are in need of less sweeping. Oh sure, the Sweeper people will curse my name, but have no fear my minions, for I am strong, and resilient, and most importantly...CRUMB FREE! Please note: this does not include crumb cake, for crumb cake is delicious and should never be forbidden. Only mothers shall be allowed to eat the crumb cake.

September 30

I can honestly say that I've never prayed (or cursed!) so much in my life, before I became a mother. I am sure you are familiar with the phrase, "There are no atheists in fox holes." Well, the same goes for parenthood. Even if you never believed before, you will find yourself praying, wishing, HOPING that there is a being greater than yourself that will help your child PUT A CORK IN IT! First you will pray...then you will cuss...pray, then cuss. Maybe cuss a prayer on occasion. It's not pretty, but it has been known to happen.

It starts about day two of their life, when the realization hits you that these suckers don't sleep. They neverrrrr sleep. And that is when the prayers begin..."Please GOD, let him sleep!", "Dear God, please! PLEASE! I will never ask for anything else...for a while"...which quickly turns into, "I WILL NEVER ASK FOR ANYTHING BUT SLEEP EVER AGAIN AS LONG AS WE BOTH SHALL LIVE, AMEN!"

I am telling you, I was praying so hard at some points that I swear I was levitating!!! I was visualizing Jesus himself,

laying hands on that baby and working his Son of God
mojo to get that little dude to sleep!!! Hate to say it, but at
two years old, I'm STILL saying these prayers! It's like he
is allergic to sleep. He wakes screaming about three times
every night. I'm feeling like a ... okay, fine, MORE of a
lunatic! Thank God (see, here we go again!) I don't have
access to sedatives, because I can tell you that ONE of us
would be taking them!

I look forward to the day when my son is fifteen, and I
randomly go into his room 2-3 times per night and scream
at the top of my lungs. That's gonna be a hoot! And good
birth control, for I shall remind him of these days
foreverrrrrr! "Hey son, like to sleep? Then make sure you
keep it in your pants!" Yeah, it's okay...you can steal that
line. :)

October 1

I've made no secret about my hatred of hot fries. While at
the mall today, I came to the conclusion that while hot
fries are evil, corn dogs are the devil! TOO DAMN HOT
FOR TOO DAMN LONG! It's like nuclear hot. Needs to
be a weapon. Serve corn dogs to the Taliban. There is

something about that outer bread shell that keeps that heat in for an unearthly amount of time! Take a look in the food court next time you are at the mall and you will see table after table of mothers who are blowing themselves into hyperventilation, trying to cool these freakin' things! It is the one thing that kids gravitate towards and yet you know that there are fits and crying in your immediate future. The kids get real upset, too. ;) But seriously, how many times have you ordered the dogs, then immediately started saying, "Ok now, they will have to cool. Don't touch. HOT! Owies! No, no! Not yet! Gotta cool! HOT! Gotta blow!" And then you proceed to singe the skin right off of your fingertips, while trying to release that lava-hot heat! And the blowing. MY GOD the BLOWING!!! "Hoooo, hoooooo, hoooooo, not yet, hoooooo, hooooo, still too hot, baby, hoooo, hooooo, stop crying, hoooo, hooooo, almost ready, hooooo, hoooo, I know you're hungry, hoooo, hooooo, mama's dizzy..." I suggest that they keep some pre-cooked corn dogs under a heat lamp like the rest of the fast food world, and let everyone hold on to their skin! As a mother I say amen and hallelujah! Or better yet, pack a pb&j next time and call it a day! #lukewarmrocks

October 3

I have a serious pet peeve...made up words like 'spooktacular' or 'souptastic', 'imagymnation'! Drives me NUTS! But for some reason, any word followed by 'palooza' makes me giggle. Why is that? Gigglepalooza. :) There's no way you can say that and NOT smile! NO WAY! See what I just did? I am wielding my power because at this very moment you are sitting there, trying to say 'gigglepalooza' with a straight face. Am I right? GOTCHA!

October 6

Consider this a public service announcement to fathers. A PSA-palooza, if you will. Papa-looza? ~insert giggles here~ No, wait. That sounds too much like papa is a looza. lol No sense name calling. I digress.

The life this information saves could be your own. ARE YOU LISTENING?! Good! As mothers, we think of everything. EV-ER-Y-THING! We think of it forwards, backwards, and four months in advance, then we tie it up with a bow that coordinates with the outfit we plan on wearing that day, once we get just the right shoes to make it pop. We develop alternate scenarios complete with the locations of all the exits and the nearest hospitals. We've memorized traffic patterns, migratory birds, and the latest flavors of Slurpee's on rotation at the local gas station. We've got Benadryl, baby wipes, extra snacks, and the immunization card stashed, just in case. What? You don't know what the scenario is yet? OF COURSE YOU DON'T, you aren't a MOTHER! The short answer is...IT DOESN'T MATTER WHAT THE SCENARIO IS, we've got it covered! We've got next year's birthday party all mapped out and know what this year's hot Christmas gifts are going to be. I know it is July. That's my point!

So, you know how sometimes you come home and hit us with an idea that has just popped into your head? How your voice goes up an octave and you have an intense sense of urgency because fear has gripped your heart that details haven't been covered? For example, "We aren't going to have enough room for everyone to sit at the party!," "Christmas Eve is TOMORROW!," "Who's going to watch the kids Saturday night?," just to name a few. You know how we roll our eyes and give a heavy sigh? Yeah well, imagine if we walked into your office at work and started spouting our big plans for your major project that you've been working on for months, that's due tomorrow. Yeah, it's like that. Capeesh? This is our office. We realize you are half owner in this investment, however, give Mama the bennie o' the doubt because nine times out of ten, we've got it covered. Now just stand there, look pretty, and hand over the paycheck, sweetheart. :) #whostheboss

T's and P's

October 8

The Laws of Child Rearing dictate that the child with the
extreme heat sensitivity shall be the one to cry and insist
on wearing long sleeves and fleece-lined Crocs in the
middle of summer. She will then be found running around
in the backyard in 90 degree heat. This Law also states
that the child with walking pneumonia and bronchitis will
refuse to wear shoes and a jacket. Why? Because it is the
Law. We don't ask why. Do not anger the Law. It's a lot
like the rhythm...it'll get ya!

This is all hypothetical, of course. All of it. In fact, I'm just hypothetically a mom. I'm actually sitting in the quad with my backpack, waiting for the chem lab to open. I'm just making up all of these stories because I am bored. Bored with all of the free time and quiet around me. These dang leaves, rustling in the trees. And the freakin' chirpy birds are just annoying. Oh, what I wouldn't give to have a couple of kids running around, screaming and fighting. A little hair-pulling might be nice. Aaaahhhh, someday. For now I just have to deal with staying up as late as I want, sleeping in, parties, midnight movies. Boriiiiiing. Can't wait until I have little kids and I can stay at home in my pajamas all day, watching TV, eating bonbons. Maybe then I will be able to gain some weight. I am so sick of looking like a stick figure. I am just a bean pole and I hate it. No matter how much I eat, I just can't seem to gain any weight! And it isn't like I work out, either. I do hardly any exercise! But someday I will be a mom, relaxing at home with my sweet babies, and have a curvier figure. That will be awesome! Oops! There's the bell...gotta go! #hopethiszitisgonebyfridaynight P.S. It's ok to want to slap her. #assisnowthesizeofabarn

October 9

Heaven knows I enjoy social networking as much as the next guy. Maybe even MORE than the next guy. After all, it is what keeps me connected with the outside world while currently living my life of home exile. #sequesteredisafourletterword

See, I would never have known about my little # guys that bring me so much joy, if not for social networking. And it is a fantastic way to get information out to a bunch of people at once. I like keeping myself informed of what is going on in my friends' lives and being able to offer 'likes,' commentary, and 'thoughts and prayers.' Which brings me to an important subject.

This may be a sensitive topic, and some may take offense, but I consider myself a Global Messenger and this subject needs to be addressed. I'm talking about 'thoughts and prayers.' The comment we all leave when someone posts a status that tells of trial and tribulations in one's own life, or within their family and close friends. I am so happy and willing to offer 'thoughts & prayers.' It is a wonderful gesture, and I do it with joy, always...often...sometimes...

okay, not always. Here's the problem, there are some...
not naming names...who ALSO see themselves as a Global
Messenger. But instead of providing random crap and
information to the masses, which is the role I play, they
are the Global Messengers of all things tragic. I shall call
them the Global Messengers of Doom. Their status
updates not only reflect the pain and hardship of their own
lives, their families, their neighbors, but the hardships of
cousins of their neighbors, neighbors of cousin's neighbor
who went to school with the neighbor of another cousin
whose dog was run over while trying to help a blind
neighbor cross the street. Or was it the blind cousin...I'm
confused. It reminds me of the local evening news and
how, if there isn't anything super sad and tragic in your
own 100 mile radius, or even your state, they will travel
3,000 miles to tell you about a family of chipmunks who
was eaten by a pit bull. That is how you know it is a slow
news day.

I'm all for handing out 'thoughts & prayers,' don't get me
wrong. But I consider myself a sensitive sort who really
takes these stories to heart. And my heart can only take so
much before going into overload. Then I run the risk of
not feeling sincere in my 'thoughts and prayers,' but more

numb. I can handle sharing the burden for my fellow man, but there is a point where it becomes ridiculous. There is so much tragedy in this world and I really can't handle hearing stories from people, about people, that they don't even know but have only vaguely heard about. I start out with the best of intentions, but after the eighth horror post in a week, I'm reduced from "I'm so sorry. My thoughts and prayers are with your family!" to "Sorry. Thoughts and prayers" to "t's and p's." It's like the energy has just been sucked out of me!

I think it is guilt that makes me comment on such sad stories, but I just don't have the energy to completely type out "thoughts and prayers." It's kind of like the story of the boy who cried wolf. When the same people post over and over about tragic stories, I wonder if they just stay in a state of depression over all of this news, or if they are in some way wanting attention for themselves by posting. I don't know but I just don't understand it. So, as the Global Messenger I will warn you, if you find yourself getting lots of 't's & p's' on your posts, you might be at risk of becoming a Global Messenger of Doom.

I say we apply a rule of Three Degrees of Separation for

t's & p's. If the tragedy isn't within three degrees of you, then leave the request for t's & p's to someone else. Like my grandma used to say, "you don't have to tell everything you know." You can put in a request for an aunt or an uncle, a cousin, neighbor, or even a neighbor's immediate relative, but then you MUST STOP! And DOGS DON'T COUNT! I love dogs, but come on! Pray for your own damn dog. #thetruthhurts

October 12

It's not that I'm not a morning person. Well, yes it is. I'm more of a mid-morning person. That's when I really shine. :) But I can handle things fine early in the morning as long as I'm not being immediately peppered with 4,000 questions and requests. Unfortunately, Bubba wakes up with things he needs to say at rapid-fire speed. "Hi Mommy! I go poopies. Is a mess. Bone? (granola bar) Muck? (Milk) Fowers! (Flowers on my robe) Sissy? Daddy take shower? Chickens? (He wants to watch the movie *Rio*) Pants? (wants to get dressed) Go bye-bye? Pawk? (Park) Gy? (Gym) Juice? Waaaaataaaaaah! (the punch line to 'What is Bruce Lee's favorite drink?)" The previous questions were all delivered in less than a minute. Each

with a pause, waiting for my response. He's been up for
five minutes and I'm exhausted!

For those that are saying, "just ignore him," I'd like to
invite you to come over and meet Bubba. There is no
ignoring him. To quote a very famous movie line, he
"won't be IGNORED!" He is relentless and determined.
Good qualities in a successful adult, but annoying as hell
in a child. He will keep asking, and asking, and asking,
until you answer him. And not just any answer! It must
be the one he wants to hear! "Mommy, go pawk? (park)
Mommy? Mommy? Go pawk? Mommy?" No, Bubba.
Not today. "Mommy? Mommy? Go pawk? Pawk?
Mommy?" Mommy ignores. So he says even LOUDER,
"Mommy? Mom? Mommy? Pawk? Go Pawk Mommy?"
Experience has taught me that this is NOT the time to go
sit down on the couch, for this determined child will climb
into my lap, take my hands in his face and nose to nose he
will say, "Mommy. Mommy? Go pawk, Mommy? Pawk?
Mommy?" And this will go on all day. I have tried
everything under the sun and just realized that it is who
this child is and until he is old enough for me to send him
to his room alone, I will have to continue going about my
business and pretend I don't hear him. That won't

dissuade him from continually asking, pecking me to death like a chicken. But it is either pretend or go into the Ugly Mommy Voice and threaten to rip his arm off and beat him with it. I try to avoid that as much as I possibly can. I guarantee you that by naptime my nerves will be absolutely RAW!!!! It is cruel and unusual punishment, I tell ya! #calgoncantfixthis #amiallowedtocallcpsonmyself

October 15

Remember back to when you first started dating? How just eating in front of your beloved made you a nervous wreck? Okay, obviously I'm not talking to the men out there. They'll eat in front of anyone or anything. But for us girls, especially when we are young, everything is embarrassing. If someone would have told me then that I would some day be married and having extensive, in-depth conversations about poop on a daily basis, I would have crawled into a hole and wanted to die!

It begins slowly, during pregnancy. At first you are too embarrassed to tell your beloved about the interesting and often disgusting things that are occurring with your body. Fearing on some level that he will never want to touch you again. And then one night when you are about seven months pregnant you meet another couple for dinner. You have a lovely time while they are gushing about your 'glow' and how cute you look with your pregnant belly. Awww shucks. ~bats lashes~ As you are walking to your car, holding hands with the father of your child with all of your glowingness, the other couple follows closely behind. You are sharing stories, exchanging jokes, when all of a sudden, out of nowhere...pbththth. wtf. Thank God for traffic noise. Maybe they didn't hear. But they were right behind you! It was so shocking, and so sudden that you can't help but giggle as you get to the car. You have to share it with your husband because it was as if it happened to someone else, it was THAT unexpected and out of the blue. You blame it on the baby. The baby made you do it. And who can be grossed out by a baby, right? I mean, this is all totally hypothetical, of course. Actually, it happened to a friend of mine. Really. But this is the beginning of what will soon be referred to as The Bowel Years.

By the time you are nine months pregnant you are so OVER IT, that you think you might actually be under it. You are uncomfortable and ready to get this kid OUT! If you have to endure the trials and tribulations of the last months of pregnancy, then dammat, hubby is going to at least have to hear about it! And since he is the one who got you into this mess, you really don't care if it grosses him out and he never wants to touch you again! In fact, at some point you may even inform him that he will never touch you again. This is about the same stage when you don't care if this kid comes out sideways, just GET OUT! I have a feeling that this sentiment is practice for when they are 25 and still living in your basement playing video games. (I know, I know. I live in California and we don't have basements, but it makes the story better, doesn't it? For some reason, the visual of a grown man living in his parents' basement is just funnier than him living in his upstairs bedroom. Unless of course you ACTUALLY have a grown son in your basement. That shit isn't funny at all and my heart goes out to you.) #t's&p's

Now back to the poop! It really gets interesting when the baby arrives and you are told that their poop will start out one color and then change within a few days. And then depending on if you are nursing or formula feeding, it will take on an even different color. So you wait...you analyze, you call in your spouse for second opinions, debate on calling the doctor for a third opinion. Should we save it?

Take a pic? Where's my phone? Oh yeah, I'm not kidding either. Not trying to be funny. It just IS funny.
Here's a true story for ya...when hubby and I were dating, my best friend and her husband invited us over to their house. When we knocked on the door, she opened with a big smile and very excitedly said, "Come in! Come look! The baby just pooped and it looks like peanut butter! Isn't that funny?! Derek is videotaping it!" I. Shit. You. Not. True story. I was ready to initiate a serious intervention. Something was wrong with these people. I would learn a few years later that it is just the newborn parents' learning curve. It is all so wondrous and miraculous that even poop is a major event!

"Honey, I'm home" is soon followed by "did he poop today?", "how much?", "how many times?", "what color?" I'm sorry to be the one to tell you if you didn't already know, but it's going to happen. I think this may be the best birth control and abstinence support we can give our teenagers. If we explain to them that when they have babies they will be having conversations all day long about poop, I think it will put a stop to their shenanigans. Then we will whip out the 'projectile poop' stories and seal the deal. #scaredstraigh

October 17

I was taught at an early age that a reputation is very important. Work hard to maintain a good reputation because that is all you have. Be honest, have integrity, and work hard. I think this is especially important for young girls. I bet right now you can think of the girl in your high school who had a bad reputation. Sidebar...why don't I remember any BOYS with bad reputations? I must explore this further...now back to our regularly scheduled program. We all assumed the rumors were true, but do we really know? I'm sure there are many who never did what people say they did. In fact, wasn't there just a movie about that?

So work hard, I did. I was proud to be a cheerleader, even though our school never won any games. Cheering for a losing team built character! I studied hard, got good grades, worked, and was Senior Class President. Went on to college to get my degree, and I remember one night, not long after graduation, when a very good looking guy approached me and a group of my friends. We started talking and had so much in common. We laughed, exchanged smart-ass commentaries (who ME?) and had a great time. As I was leaving, he asked if I'd like to go out to dinner with him some time. Sounded nice. Before I could answer, he handed me his card. His last name was Cherry. Cherry. Really? Really. And my name is Shari. Shari Cherry...Shari...Cherry. And you know the date would be amazing. He'd be the best thing since sliced bread and have a mansion on the hill with a full-time masseuse on staff. I could sit in the shade all day and sip mimosas while having a mani/pedi. (Why is this not sounding so bad to me right now? Reputation shmation! lol I kid! I kid! Or do I...) This all flashed through my mind in an instant. He was going to be fabulous because God has a sense of humor. And after all of my hard work all those years, trying to obtain and maintain a good reputation, I was going to be labeled a stripper for the rest of my life. I mean, just call me a slut and get it over with, why don't ya?! We'd have two kids, Carrie and Gary, a dog named Maraschino, and our cat, Bing. Our Christmas cards would say, "Have a Merry Cherry Christmas!" Oh the horror!

I have no idea how long I stood there, in a stupor, with these images running through my mind. When I came to, I politely smiled and handed him his card back. "I'm sorry" was all I could muster, and I walked away. I'm sure he picked up the pieces and moved on with his life. But then again...maybe not. #datingsthepits ;)

October 20

Once upon a time, there was a grocery store executive who had a brainstorm. "Let's get little grocery carts for the KIDS to push around! They can follow Mommy around and help her! It will keep the kids close by and keep them occupied!" This man was not a father. I know it was a man who came up with this idea because no MOTHER would EVER come up with this crazy-ass idea. If he was a father, his children lived in Antarctica and he saw them for six hours, twice a year. I know I don't even have to explain to most of you why this is the worst idea in the history of bad ideas, you probably have the scars to prove it, but please humor me. If only I could have been in on that meeting with Mr. GroceryMan, in my current mental state. Oh what fun I would have had. Here goes...

"First of all sir, let me walk you through what that shopping experience would be like for not only the mother of these children, but also for all of the employees and fellow customers. As the mother enters the store and selects a cart for herself and a little cart for each of her children...what? Yes, I said EACH. The average parent has 2.5 children, and each child and a half will need their very own cart. Because they will, sir. Because they will. Because. Because they are kids. Just because they WILL, okay? I don't make the rules, sir. I'm just telling you that these are the laws of childhood and I promise you that even that little halfer of a kid is going to want his own cart! Sir, we haven't even made it in the store yet! Can I continue? Thank you.

Okay, so mom and kids all have their carts now. Let's start in the produce section. Everyone is going to want to start throwing shit...ummm...sorry, I will try to control my language, it is just the visual is overwhelming me at the moment...I'll pull it together...okay, so the little angels are going to want to immediately start filling their carts. No, this is not good news because Mama ain't gonna pay for all of the random crap these kids throw in there! Money doesn't grow on trees! And where will these little hands be able to reach? The bottom row of the peaches and apples, that's where! House of cards comes to mind. 'CLEAN UP IN PRODUCE!' and they've been in the store for three minutes. Let's move on, shall we? Because now it is time to see what these carts are made of! Can they go zero to fifteen in three seconds? Why yes, I believe they can! So now you have these little hoodlums running up and down the aisles RACING, severing the Achilles tendon of every poor soul who gets in their way! They are knocking over displays and running over toes, as their mother is trying to ward off the aneurism that is beckoning and has started cussing a blue streak that she wore sandals and not shoes with better traction for taking the corners. It is a constant stream of 'NO! Do NOT put that in your cart! NO! NO! Because! Because I am your MOTHER and I say NO!' God forbid she needs to go down the cereal or cookie aisle. Grocery shopping is hard enough on a mom without adding this level of difficulty. Do me a favor, take my two kids grocery shopping and get back to me on this. Oh sure, the KIDS will want to shop in your store but last I checked, they didn't have a job! Make life easier on Mom and you will change the world." ~cue the angels~ #grocerychildrenshouldbeseenandnotfelt #shariforpresident

Leave Me a Grocery Cart, Skippy

October 23

As you know, I'm a new kindergarten mom. This has come with lots of new revelations. For example, my daughter informed me that "the backpack goes on my back, Mom. That is why it has straps. Put it on me and now hold my hand. That is how you walk your child to kindergarten." Ummm...okay. Although, even at five years old, as soon as we got inside the gate where all the kids were she announced, "Mom, you need to let go of my hand now." Ummm..okay. Once she was on the playground, I kissed her good-bye. Bossy McBosserson, Professional

Kindergartener, informed me that "we should go say hello
to the yard duty lady before you go." Who is this child?

Upon picking her up from school, she immediately
thanked me for taking her to kindergarten. She said, "My
teacher is so sweet! I didn't know she was going to be
SWEET!" We then moved on to the fact that "worms live
in wet dirt...and soil. It's true." Way to hit the ground
running, teacher!

Another revelation that hit me as I was leaving the school
grounds was that apparently I am supposed to be carrying
my coffee with me. I'm not talking about paper cups with
lids, from the coffee store. I'm talking about big honkin'
MUGS of coffee, or tea because there were a few dangling
bags that I observed. Honkin' mugs o' coffee. And these
were women who were dropping off older kids so they
were on the campus for all of about two and a half
minutes. You couldn't leave your coffee in the car?
Really? In fact, you couldn't leave your coffee at your
house, which is within a five-mile radius? Gotta have the
coffee right there on this August morning with a
temperature of 80 degrees at 8 a.m., in case you catch a
chill? I guess no harm done, just found it funny that there

was not just one, but SEVERAL coffee muggers. Like it was a club or a clique or something. Maybe I misunderstood and it is a drip-off instead of a drop-off. Maybe they were the 'green' coffee drinkers, like the anti-water bottle people. Don't want to harm the environment so gonna bring my MUG! Who knows, next year I might be right there with them, scoffing at the new, non-hydrated, gonna-catch-their-death-of-cold, newbies. #mugsarethenewblack

October 27

Have you ever worn a bathing suit top under your sundress on a day when you need to run to the store but don't feel like doing your hair or makeup? As if to say to those who might scoff at your lack of grooming, "I am on my way to/coming back from the pool and needed a few things real quick." Oh. Yeah, me neither. I just heard about someone who does that and thought it was completely ridiculous. I mean, really. Who DOES that? ~looks around nervously~ Although, let's think this through. She might have a good point. It is a busy day with the kiddos and you have no other plans, but discover that you are out of milk. Now while you were happy to have 10 minutes to shower, you have discovered that there is no time to dry the hair or put on makeup, for fear that the rugrats will destroy the place and dismantle the entertainment center for their own entertainment. A bathing suit peeking out of the top of a sundress looks very beachy! And how many of us have actually run into the store on the way home from the beach or pool?! THAT'S RIGHT! We all have! And there's no shame in looking beachy! This may not be an issue in a big city, but in a small town, I can GUARANTEE you are going to run into at least three people that you haven't seen in 25 years on the days when you are looking like a drowned rat! Now, instead of word going around town that 'Shari is a hot mess,' it is 'Oh, I saw Shari at the store and she was looking breezy!' :D

I guess now the cat's out of the bag. It's me. I do this. And now my secret is out. My mom commented to me one day and asked if I'd just come from the pool. Nope. Just a ruse to confuse!

And hey, gym gear also works! Workout top and pants, running shoes, ponytail, give the whole Sporty Spice vibe!

But don't add jewelry! Jewelry may give the impression that you are trying. Do not try. Do, or do NOT! I go full hag or I don't go hag at all.

#trainwreckscanbemanaged

October 29

All of this talk of grocery stores got me to thinking...would it be possible for my grocery store to leave at least a few carts in the parking lot? They have probably 400 carts and every ten minutes they send Skippy out to collect them. Mothers with small children need carts close to the car! Especially those of us with BIG children. Thirty pounds is a lot of Bubba to haul across the parking lot, while carrying the shopping cart cover, and a purse, and holding the hand of Sissy! I'm ready to have a little chitty-chat with Mr. Groceryman, promising to not think poorly of his managerial skills if there are five or six shopping carts in the cart return.

On a few occasions, I have pulled into a parking spot and seen one or two carts, and been so excited! Only to see Skippy heading for the cart return. Oh crap! For the love of God, NOOOOOO! As quickly as I can, I am unbuckling and racing him to the carts. He knows I want that cart and he is eyeing me suspiciously. He is bound and determined to beat me. Not today, Skippy! NOT. TODAY! I can appreciate his desire to be efficient, but come on! #iwillwhoopyourasskid

November 2

As mothers, we get very few quiet moments in our life. One quiet moment occurs when pumping gas. At least it USED to be quiet. Kids are in the car, doors are closed, screams are muffled, and all we would hear is the clicking of the gas pump...until now. Some mental giant came up with the idea of installing televisions above the gas pump. But not just any television, one that only plays commercials and advertisements! Like we aren't bombarded enough with media, now we have to endure the constant yacking of Mr. Fake Gasoline Scientist Man. How do I know he is a fake, you ask? Because he is a cop on one of my Tuesday night shows! And now you've gone and ruined my four and a half minutes of peace! Are we really so pitiful that we can't stand and pump gas without some sort of electronic stimulation? Gone are the days of standing in relative peace and quiet, enjoying the breeze and the slight buzz you get from the fumes. Party's over, people.

So I pump my gas and move on to the car wash portion of the program. I used to go to a touchless carwash in my old neighborhood. I didn't realize what a special treat that was until I was subjected to the violent car beating that awaited me at my local gas station. I don't know about you, but I have found that a little soap and a powerful spray of water does the trick. It's like magic! You don't have to beat the dirt to death like you're taking down Sasquatch! #ificouldruntheworld

November 5

Dear coffee barista, while I appreciate the fact that you would like to give me my money's worth, MUST YOU filleth my cup so full that it spills down the side of the mug when you put the lid on it? Because now my cup is sticky... and mama has enough sticky in her life. And the coffee that seeps out onto the top of the lid is destined to wind up

in my lap adding yet another stain to my fabulous
wardrobe. Although, I shouldn't just blame the baristas
because this seems to happen to me in the drive-thru with
my soda, and when I take the kids for smoothies.
NEWSFLASH! I'm not going to report you to the company
for leaving me a quarter of an inch of breathing room at
the top of my cup! Promise, I won't! I think the school
moms might be on to something.
#imgonnaneedabiggermug

November 7

The gym is an interesting place. Lots to observe at the
gym. Sometimes TOO much to observe. TMI, if you will...
or in this case, TMO (Too Much Observed!) I am, of
course, referring to the locker room. Where to begin. So
many problems, so little time. Now, I'm all for women
feeling good about themselves. God knows I can't stand
the whiners. But MUST we frolic in the locker room butt
nekkid? Must we? Really? Can't find a towel to wrap
around all of that loveliness?

Now some gyms are worse than others. I find, in my vast

experience, that gyms in the higher income areas house more nekkids than others. True story. I guess they figure if they paid that much for their parts, they want to show it off. I suppose they have a point...or two. ;)

I have discovered that there are many women who like to walk around nekkid, talking on their cell phones, drinking coffee, chatting and making other women very uncomfortable. This sort of behavior caught me completely unaware and took some getting used to. Ok, fine! I never got used to it! So sue me! Prudy McPrude, I am not. If you happen to be nekkid while disrobing or getting dressed, big whoop! Nobody should be looking at you, if they have any manners. I thought the unspoken rule of the locker room was, you go in, head down, handle your bizness, move on! Well, allow me to enlighten you in case you don't already know, but this is not always the case. There are LOTS of nekkid talkers. Oh, they will ask you questions...LOTS of questions. And your polite nature will make you want to look at them when you are speaking. But then you end up with this bug-eyed stare because you are tryyyyying, straaaaaaaining not to glance down at the horror before you. Because even though these ladies frequent the gym...umm, how shall I say...you wouldn't know it. Maybe they have fantastic cardio vascular capabilities, who knows. And I think it is great they are there and feel comfy about themselves. Yeehaw for them! Really! But it is just the most awkward feeling. All I can hear, as I'm trying to focus on their FACE and maintain my train of thought, is my five-year old saying, "Awkwarrrrrrd!"

I was trying to avoid a conversation just yesterday as I overheard the nekkids talking about the music at the gym. A song came on and they all started singing in nekkid unison. I'm moving like the WIND, trying to wrangle my towel, and quite frankly, get the HELL out of there! I know the song they are singing and I don't like where the conversation is headed. "I love this song!" one of them said. "Me, too!" says her friend. "Who sings it?" says another. Oh dear God, no. Please, no. Make me invisible...make me invisible...please don't ask me...they're gonna ask me...sweet baby Jesus, give me strength...I can't do it with a straight face...I can't...here it comes...oh crap! "Excuse me, do you know who sings this song?" My heart is in my throat. My face has lost all color. Oh the horror! They are all looking at me with their innocent little grandma, nekkid eyes...GULP. I couldn't escape it so I took a deep breath and answered, "Bare Nekkid Ladies," and I ran from the room. I am sure the woman in the shower next to me was curious as to why there was a woman giggling and snorting by herself. I mean really, what are the ODDS of that song coming on? Just proves that God has a sense of humor.

I used to work at a gym as a massage therapist. At this particular gym, the massage rooms were at the back of the ladies' locker room. Oh joy. So every hour I am back and forth across that place, removing old sheets and adding new ones to the massage table. I made it a habit to keep my head down and just go about my business. "See no evil, see no evil" was my motto. But there was one particular nekkid lady who was absolutely in looooove with herself. You could just tell. She wanted to be noticed! She would walk around that locker room on her phone, or chatting with other non-nekkid ladies for hours! Hours! I kid you not! I'd see her on my way into the massage room, and an hour later WHOMP! There she is! Still there...still going...still nekkid. I often wondered why one of the non-nekkid ladies didn't ask her to put on some clothes. They were probably afraid of a nekkid confrontation. Nobody wants that. They probably feared she would gather up her nekkid posse (I said POSSE! Behave.) ;) and terrorize them for wearing clothes.

I remember the first time I saw this woman. I was walking around the corner into the locker room and caught a full frontal shot of her coming right towards me. I'm going to try to be as delicate as you know I can be, when I describe what has now haunted me for ten years. For you see, this woman had enhancements. Floatation devices, if you will. It was like two recreational vehicles had parked themselves on her chest. Too each his own. Whatever blows your skirt up or fills out your top! That wasn't the most shocking thing in the world to me. I mean, I DO live in Southern California. What WAS shocking, and what I was completely unaware of, was what happens to RV's as a woman ages. Think melted wax. (Sorry, I know you weren't prepared for that. Do you need a moment to recover? It's okay, take all the time you need. I'll wait...)

Imagine if you will, a wax museum...during a heat wave in the middle of August, and now the power's gone out and things are starting to...drip. Now, the actual RV's aren't movin.' Those suckers are staying put until the end of time. Grandma is gonna have some perky ta-ta's, that's fo' sho'! But you see, the skin surrounding the ta-ta's is fully aware of the age of that body. Mr. Gravity and Mother Nature are doin' what they do. I believe when I first laid eyes on this scene I let out an audible, "WHOA!" and averted my eyes. I may or may not have jerked my head to the side to protect my psyche from the bombardment that was before me. I'm not proud of it, but I think it might have happened. Yeah, so Titty Galore is comin' at me and the skin around those things is sagging...or melting...or something. All I could think was, 'For heaven's sake, woman, find your humanity and GRAB A TOWEL!' Nobody needs to see that. Although from her behavior, I have a feeling a lot of people have. Now this was ten years ago so I can ONLY imagine...although I'm trying not to... what those puppies must look like today. Wrangle those suckers into a supportive undergarment and call it a day. I BEG YOU! #whentatasattack

Bubba Sees Dead People

November 8

Hubby and I have been watching a lot of the ghost shows
on television lately. There must be at least five different
shows about hunting down ghosts, or shows where
celebrities tell their own ghost stories. Of course, I have to
explain to Hubby who most of these 'celebrity' people are.
It is a combination of him not knowing/caring and my
brain that holds on to all trivial pop culture information.
Truly, I have a gift. It only serves me in casual
conversation, but it is there. Probably makes me look like
I watch too much television, but I swear that isn't the case.

My life is spent watching the same animated movies over and over...and over four more times. I don't know where it comes from, but I'm just able to retain this trivial stuff.

Anywho, so one night we're watching one of these ghost shows and we decide it's time for bed. JUST as we lay down, Bubba decides that it is scream-thirty and proceeds to cry and cry and cry. Nothing new, he seems to cry every night at about 10:30 pm. This night, I just can't take it. He needs to SHUT IT, and shut it NOW! So I go in and get him and take his little screamer butt downstairs. It is the first time I've done this since he was a baby, but I just can't take it anymore. We sit on the couch for about ten minutes watching a show about fish, or fish hunters, or something. (Is there no end to these shows?!) After ten minutes, he decides he wants to play. Go for it, kid. Just don't scream. I go into the kitchen to get a drink and he comes running in, clinging to me like a monkey. He's never done it quite like this before. He's pointing at the door and saying, "The man! The man!" I pick him up and he is hugging me so tightly with his arms and his legs. I turn on all the lights and walk over to the door to show him that nobody is there. He seems scared so I take him into the living room and try to loosen his kung fu grip from my neck. He decides to start playing again and then suddenly he stops and looks up. Like he is looking at someone. I shit you not. Then he comes running back to me, crawls up on the couch, and says, no...he WHISPERS...my child NEVER whispers, so this is new. He whispers, "Mom, he's coming! He's coming!" Ummmm OK! I DO NOT need to hear this! NO bueno, cowboy! Negatory, good buddy! Whispering kids are creepy! His favorite cars are in his sister's play stroller and he won't touch them. I hug him and tell him nobody is there (HA!) and after a few minutes he goes back to his toys...but he still won't touch them. Ok, mama's taking some deep breaths at this point.

I should explain that ever since my grandpa passed in 1997, I've had a few experiences where I have seen him, we may or may not have spoken to each other, and in general I know when he is around. So I am pretty sure that if someone is there in my living room, it is my grandpa. I don't have any negative feelings that it is a bad or dangerous spirit, just the normal nerves when you think that your baby boy is 'seeing dead people'. I'm sure you can relate, right? Eeek! So Bubba is doing this several more times, the running back and forth between me and his toys that he won't touch. He keeps whispering, "He's coming!", and finally I have to say, "Okay son, you HAVE TO stop saying that! PLEASE!"

Trying to calm him down, I say, "You don't have to be scared. That is Mommy's Papa. He loves you. He won't hurt you." Well, mentioning 'Papa' sends Bubba into a fit of baby Tourette's where he starts blurting about Papa. "Where's Papa?", "Where's Amma?", because he thinks I'm talking about HIS Papa. So I change my tactic and start calling my Papa, 'Pop.' I say, "No baby, that is Pop. He loves you. Don't be afraid."

I will say he acted more shy, instead of afraid. Like when somebody new, that they don't know, comes over and they hide behind you a bit. Although Bubba has never been shy around anyone before, but I guess when you see a ghost it can cause you to act a little out of character. Well, we end up going to bed after about a half hour of this. I rocked him and sang some nice old church hymns before laying him down, and then he slept the rest of the night without incident.

I told Hubby about the whole ordeal in the morning. I believe I started the story with the phrase, "You would have shit. Your. Pants!" I'm nothing if not eloquent. I get a call that morning from my sister, saying that on her way home from work she got the overwhelming feeling that she needed to come over. She said it was so strong that she actually almost cried, worried that something was wrong. I told her what happened and so she came over and we walked the house, burning sage, sweet grass, praying, hopping on one leg, doing a rain dance and the hokey pokey, for good measure. We just wanted to make sure that there wasn't anybody else 'hanging' around my house. I assumed, and really felt like it was my grandpa, but I wasn't sure...until...oh yeah people, it gets better! I found a little picture of my grandparents. Bubba had never seen it before. I knelt down and showed it to him and asked, "Who is that?" He points to my grandpa and says, "Pop!"

I looked at my sister. "Did you hear that?" "Clear as a bell," she said. Now I just can't help but show him the picture every few days and ask who that is. I get such a kick out of it. He didn't know my grandma because he asks, "Who's that?" I think when she passed, she was so ready to go that she high-tailed it out of here and never looked back. I've never really felt her around, like I do my grandpa.

So I had a little chat with Pop and told him that I'm happy that he's watching over my kids, but please stop scaring the beegeezus out of them. Mama's got enough on her plate. Unless of course, he babysits!!
#desperatetimescallfordesperatemeasures

November 11

Well, my gym days might be numbered! Some little heathen BIT BUBBA in the gym daycare THREE TIMES!! Like baby freakin' Edward Cullen! Bit him so hard that it broke the skin and you can see every little tooth mark! There's even a hickey in the middle where he sucked on it. I'm telling you, if I would have seen that, I don't know if I could have controlled myself from flicking that kid on the forehead to get him off of my baby! I can't believe that Bubba didn't punch him in the face, honestly. He's done much worse to his sister for much less. He must have just been in shock. The daycare girls said that the little boy was biting so fast that he got three bites in before they could get to him. By the time they came to get me, the father had left with the biter. I mean, really, what kid bites THREE TIMES?! That is a serial biter.

According to the daycare, he's done this before. Well, hear me now and believe me later, but he will NOT return to that daycare. If he does, we won't. I had to take poor little Bubba to the doctor and get him an antibiotic. Just broke my heart to hear him say, "Mama, yook! Owie! Hurrrt!" Mama bear is ready to whoop some ass! They tell me that the mother is denying that her kid would bite someone. I'd like to check her for marks because I GUARANTEE that kid has bitten her before! A kid doesn't just start biting and do it THREE TIMES! Besides, the daycare workers saw him do it. And funny that the parents rushed out of the daycare before I could get there. I went immediately when they came to get me. What is wrong with people?

So the kid is on a two week suspension until the managers have a meeting to decide whether or not to make it permanent. I'm going to be nice until they decide. Giving them the bennie o' the doubt. If they choose poorly, watch out. I can't imagine they'd want to put more kids in danger from little Twilight, especially since he's done it before. If they would have banned this blood sucker the first time, I wouldn't be dealing with this. So for now, we wait. #takeabiteoutofcrime

November 14

I am officially old. I think I heard a bell ring. Like, instead of hearing a bell ring and an angel gets his wings...I heard a bell and was offered an AARP card. (Which reminds me, *AARP, STOP sending me emails, I am NOT 65 yet!*) Okay, back to my story. So I'm walking Sissy to kindergarten and all of a sudden I hear all of this noise behind us. I turn around and there are six kids coming towards us at lightning speed, all riding their scooters and hootin' and hollerin.' I had to grab Sissy and pull her towards me so that she didn't get run over. Here's how I know that I'm old...the word "shenanigans" actually flew out of my mouth. Something like, "Oh you crazy kids and all of your shenanigans!" No joke. It's like I was an 80-year-old man living in South Jersey. I decided that the word 'shenanigans' was probably created by some such man who was up to his Depends with all of the behavior of these little hoodlums! It's the only word that describes their actions. SHENANIGANS, I tell ya!

November 15

Wanna know something? Here's some crazy toddler info that nobody but me will tell you about! Now, if you are currently pregnant, I don't know if I want you reading this quite yet. Maybe bookmark it and save it for later. Why? Because you chicks cry at the drop of a bucket and I'm not sure you can take it. (Oh geez, here you go.) Stop crying. Please. Stop. Yes, I like you! I DO like you! I never said I didn't. I didn't call you crazy. Your hormones are just wild right now. I said WILD, not CRAZY! You are not fat. I never said you were fat. You are very cute, now can we get back to my story?! Thank you. Yes, I will take you to get ice cream, just let me finish this.

Okay, so when your child is about two years old, they will go through a phase...a very lonnnnng phase...where they will ask you for something. Actually, 'ask' is too gentle of a word, they will turn into mini drill sergeants and scare the ever-lovin' crap out of you and DEMAND something. Let's use juice as an example. Ok, so mini drill sergeant will DEMAND juice so passionately that you are convinced that if you can only deliver this juice in time, they will instantly calm down and this juice will fulfill a longing deep inside of them that will complete them in such a profound way, that suddenly they will know all of their abc's, recite the Pledge of Allegiance, and be able to ride a two-wheeler. Yes, I thought this as well. But I am here to tell you that this will not be the case. I want you to be prepared dear friends, for this mini drill sergeant, upon being presented with this ice cold nectar for which they have been longing, will proceed to throw it back in your face and scream, "NO JUICE!" in their best Soup Nazi voice. For you see, now you have offended them on a deep spiritual level. Shame on you. They didn't want JUICE, they wanted CRACKERS! How could you be so dumb? Now run off and get those crackers so that they too, can be thrown in your face. It is a cycle that goes on and on and on. Ask for something, then refuse. Ask for something, then refuse. Until Mom and Dad are following junior down the rabbit hole into Crazytown. This is why mothers drink and eat lots of cookies. We drink & binge because child abuse is against the law.

When my daughter started doing this, I thought she had mental problems. Well, she did, but nothing permanent. Just the normal mental instability of a toddler. One day, in a fit of desperation, I went to a health food store to see what I could find. Some magic pill...a sedative...SOMETHING! When I came across some homeopathic kit for all sorts of children's coughs, fevers, colds and...what is this??...a pill for CALMING?! Can this be? My heart was all aflutter when I read the description of this magic pill. It said, "for contrariness, demanding something and then immediately refusing it." WHAT THE...!?! Am I on Candid Camera? I looked around cautiously because this was just too weird. The fact that someone could absolutely LABEL the hell I had been going through was amazing. Contrariness? I had never heard of such a thing and yet it described her perfectly! The weight that was lifted off my shoulders was unbelievable. There were others out there who were dealing with this kind of crazy, too! I wasn't alone! (Which then led me back to thinking of my friends with older kids...pretty much ALL of my friends...and how they never seemed to mention this little 'phase' to me either. I'm gonna be whoopin' butts for a long time, that is fo' sho.')

Well these little puppies changed my life! I'm using them again for Bubba as he has entered this lovely stage. Oh the joy. They seemed to work better on Sissy, but he's got a lot more energy so maybe I need to up the dosage to take down the beast. :) I kid, I kid! #youllneverknow

Does a Bear Shit in the Woods?

November 17

Just saw on the news that a bear attacked campers. Did you hear about this? In their tents...while they slept... attacked them! They are dead. Holy Moses, THIS is why I don't. Camp. In. Tents. I did it one time, never thinking about bears until it was almost nightfall and the other seasoned campers started using rope to haul all of our crap up into a tree. WTH?! I was sitting there, making s'mores and minding my own beeswax when my stuff started going up a tree in a sack! When they explained to me, with smiles on their faces, that the bears will come into your tent if they smell anything, even TOOTHPASTE, I could have fainted. Are ya kidding me?! WHY is this a theme in my life?! People not telling me V.I.S. (Very Important Shit!) beforehand?! BEFORE I haul myself and a 40-pound backpack into this mosquito-infested hell we call 'The Backcountry'? BEFORE I squirted eight ounces of Deet on top of my head because the swarm of mosquitos was so thick that I couldn't see!?! I was told that Deet was dangerous so use it sparingly but two hours into the hike, I welcomed death! It was at this moment that boyfriend decided to inform me that we would be hiking a 26 mile loop in four days. Really? Couldn't have MENTIONED that before today? I was under the impression that we were hiking five miles, camping for three days and heading home. I had to be back HOME in four days to start a new job, so that meant us leaving the group (15 members of his family, so that made it even more awkward) and hiking alone sans GPS. And then it started to rain. So bears + my shit in a tree + leaving the group to surge ahead and hike another 21 miles in the next three days through the wilderness + rain = Shari losing her mind. This is why I cried in a tent in the middle of nowhere all. Night. Long. This was the first clue that "boyfriend" and I weren't exactly simpatico. I cried cuz I was afeared o' the bears.

He cried cuz he was afeared o' me. We ended up hiking back out the very next day. I think he realized that if we went ahead of the group, his body might never be found. Hey Mister! You know who you are, and I know you're out there...come closer...let me give ya one more slap for old times' sake! #mustfindamanwholikesroomservice

November 23

I often refer to my home as Baby Alcatraz because we have gates and checkpoints about every ten feet. It had to be done. We resisted as long as we could but at one point I felt like I was spending half my life with my leg hiked up in the air! I would have to use it as a barrier for Bubba to keep him out of the bathroom when I was brushing Sissy's teeth...away from the oven when I'm taking dinner out... out of the pantry when I'm getting food or scrambling to get in and make a break for it! I'm sure it was quite a sight to see when I'm standing at the kitchen island, chopping veggies, and alternating legs to keep Bubba out of the cupboards. Not to mention the song that goes with it, "No Bubba! NO! Stop! Bubba, NO!" I refused to put locks on my brand new kitchen cabinets, so that meant gates. Lots and lots of gates. Now he presses his little face into the slats and screams at me. #thismuchfunshouldbeillegal

November 25

Life is about learning. Today, for instance, I learned that my little man can woof down two pieces of pizza and half of a carton of Ben & Jerry's in one sitting. (Ok, so it was one of those single serving cartons, but still!) It's right about now that you are thinking, "Hey, she's all about health." Why yes, yes I am. Now before you call the Veggie Police, this isn't an everyday occurrence, just a day where mama had had enough. Ok, well THAT is an everyday occurrence, but the pizza and ice cream is not.

I also learned that "where there's danger, there's a space ranger!" And that the phrase "all done," which is Bubba's favorite, is applicable in many situations. When we return from walking in the morning..."all done," when pulling into the driveway..."all done," going to bed..."all done," and when hanging up the phone. And last but not least, I learned that string cheese does not melt in the dryer, and that Barbie doubles as a hammer. #whoknew

November 27

I'm going to be a billionaire, just so you know. So if you want to jump on this bandwagon, better do it now. Once the billion hits, I will no longer be accepting friendship applications. :)

How will this billionaire-dom transpire, you ask? Well, I'm going to invent a Mom Holster. A holster for Moms, if you will. (Considered calling it a Momster, but that name sounded too much like 'monster', which hit too close to home. :) Thusly, the idea was aborted.) The Mom Holster, patent pending, will be designed to hold such important items as wooden spoons, teething tablets, raisins, Tylenol, Neosporin, sunblock and bean bags. Yes, bean bags. Not for play! These bean bags are serious business! Picture it, you're in the kitchen making a sandwich for your older child. Your little one sees that you are distracted, because they are cagey like that, and makes a mad dash for the electrical outlet. Because you are behind three layers of security gates and up to your elbow in peanut butter, there's no way you can make it to junior in time to swat that hand! The answer? BEAN BAGS!!! Chuck one of those suckers across the room to buy yourself some time and let junior know that mama means business! SHOCK AND AWE! Your kid gets hit with a bean bag, they are going to forget about that electrical socket, I guarantee! Bean bags don't hurt but will startle the kid and get his attention! This buys you a second or two to make it through the security checkpoints to get to him. Try your best to aim for their torso. I find that kids don't like to be hit in the face with a bean bag. STOP IT, I'M KIDDING!! (But really, they don't. ;P) I will include a target in the package for practice so mamas can hone their skills during nap time. Or maybe I'll host a workshop entitled, "Beanbags: They're not just for catching anymore." I think I'm on to something BIG here. #mamasgotgoodaim

November 29

It's no huge revelation that calling customer service ANYWHERE sucks! The wait time just to speak to a real person is often 15 minutes. But what gets me is that it takes five minutes just to get OFF of the phone with them. It's like they have abandonment issues and just can't let go. I guess they don't realize that we have been on the phone for 15 minutes longer than they have so when our call is done we are ready...to...GO!!! I sometimes want to scream, "JUST HANG UP ALREADY!!!" I guess I could hang up on them, but that feels rude, so I'd like to just say, "Thank you, goodbye" and be done with it! But no. They have to put you through all of their "Is there anything else I can help you with?" No, thanks. That's all. "Okay, it's been a pleasure to speak with you." Yeah. Thanks. Okay, bye. "If there's anything else I can help you with..." Nope. I'm good. "If you'd like to take a survey..." No, thanks. Okay now, gotta go. "Thank you for calling, Mrs. Brown." You're welcome. Reeeeally gotta run. "Have a nice day." FOR. THE. LOVE. OF. GOD!! Click.

I thought my 85-year-old grandma said some long goodbyes, "Okay, honey. Love you. Take care, baby. Okay. Call again. Love you. Come see me soon. Okay. Okay, honey. Give that baby kisses for me. Okay, honey. Love you. Okay, bye-bye. Bye-bye, baby." The above is all true. It is an actual conversation that took place every time I spoke with my grandma. You really had to plan your escape strategy. You can't just go in all willy-nilly without an exit plan. If you did, it would take an entire recon team to pull your ass out! When ending a conversation with grandma, you need to start signing off AT LEAST five minutes before you really had to go. Even then, it's risky. My recommendation...7-10 minutes of lead time. It's the smart thing to do. #goodbyeseemstobethehardestword

December 1

Second Child Syndrome. Ever heard of it? Maybe not, because I just made it up. Seems to be common knowledge in my mommy circles. Second Child Syndrome dictates that the first child won't be the hard one...and if he is, he will be the ONLY one. It states that while your first child will be difficult at times, they will be completely manageable. So much so, that you are tricked into having another. This second child will then be hell on wheels, a whirling dervish, the Tazmanian Devil, or a phrase that I borrowed and cannot take full credit for...Bubba Bin Laden. Had this child been the first born, he would have been the LAST born because Mama would not have risked the shenanigans (Oh good Lord, there it is again! Where's my walker?!) of another child if the first was this difficult! But alas, they arrive on the scene and up go the stocks at Clairol, Ben & Jerry's, and all winemakers along the California coast. But for as much trouble as they are, God knows exactly what he's doing because they are equally as cute. They are smart as a tack and know exactly when to say, "I wub you, Mommy" to save their little butts. When people coin the phrase, "That which doesn't kill you, makes you stronger," I don't think they realize it came from a mother. I'm sure it did. No doubt in my mind. Pretty sure she had a son...bet she called him Bubba...and his shenanigans forced her to eat copious amounts of cookies and ice cream, while waving around her wooden spoon, shrieking like a crazy person. (Confession: I may or may not have, at one point, eaten cookies IN my ice cream WITH my wooden spoon.)

Remember when you were growing up and you'd see the mothers at morning drop-off? Remember how crazy some of them looked? Scary, even? I no longer judge those women, for I AM those women. I could give two rat-shizzles what I look like when I take Sissy to school in the morning, or even when I go to the store. This motherhood business has just sucked the give-a-damn right out of me and I don't care who knows it!! Before I had children, I would judge women who chose to work instead of stay at home. No more! UNCLE! I get it! Doesn't mean it is for me, for all of the griping and bitching that I do, I am one of those women who just has to do it myself. For better or for worse, it's my duty. Doesn't mean I enjoy it all the time or even 50% of the time, and doesn't mean it isn't the hardest thing I've ever done. But I guess we all grow the most when dealing with difficult things. This has really stretched me as a person and I learn every day. Some days I learn that I don't like myself very much. The challenge there is to realize that each day is a new day and for all of the aggravation with children, one of the most beautiful things about them is that they are forgiving by nature. You can have the most horrendous day, go to bed with the Mommy guilt that we all know so well, and wake up to a smiling little face that's ready to start over. We just keep moving forward, doing our best, trying to learn from our mistakes and above all else, letting our children know how much they are loved.

Since school started I am finding that my need for trips to the solitude of The Pantry are fewer and far between, which is nice. But I know that it's always there when I need it. Who knows the next phase I'm in for with these kidlets. I mean, they are only five and two years old so we've only just begun. But Bubba is starting to be a better listener and mind his Mommy, and Sissy has a sweet spirit and is learning to control that 'kindergarten sass'. At least with a five-year-old, I can send her to her room so I can take a breath. I think that is all any of us really need, just a moment to take a breath. Motherhood doesn't always allow for this, and that's a big challenge. It is a non-stop train that will eat you up and spit you out if you're not careful and if you don't take care of yourself. And so for me, the next stop in my big adventure is potty training, a big boy bed, and God help me...loose teeth. She cries for three and a half days over a hangnail so I am NOT looking forward to this. Pray for me.

Virginia Woolf once said that every woman should have a room of her own. I tend to agree. Mine is the pantry, yours might be the bathroom, or the bedroom. Whatever blows your skirt up and has a lock on the door! This is the hardest and most important job we will ever do so I say, "FIND YOUR INNER PANTRY! Grab a Ding Dong in each hand and LET'S DO THIS THANG!" (I used to be a cheerleader. Don't judge me.)

See you at the carpool, folks! I'll be the one with the big mug. :)

Facebook Posts

I continue to surprise myself at the growing number of things I am no longer able to give two shizzles about. Proof positive that my give-a-damn is, in fact, busted. :)

Nothing screams "Welcome to Hell" like arriving at the pool to find a birthday party of 12 six-year-olds. Kill me now.

Sometimes it is necessary to let the defecation hit the oscillation.

What are the odds of having TWO bugs in a salad? Pretty

small, right? Because after I had eaten my ENTIRE SALAD, I saw a really...big...(gulp)...bug. :/ Odds are probably pretty slim I already ate his brother, right? RIGHT?!! This is why I should stick with fried foods.

A man who gets up in the middle of the night with a newborn is kind of like a platypus. You know they exist, you've just never met one.

I am officially skeeved. It is off the skeeve-o-meter. Had to kill three of the biggest black widow spiders that I have ever seen AND their nest. OMG. I just said 'nest'. Which is completely and totally revolting when referring to spiders. Just saying the word 'nest' makes me gag. Skeeved. Queen of the SkeeveFest. How big were they, you ask? Well, ummm...how can I put this delicately...I heard (and felt. :/ Dear Lord, help me.) them...pop. -cue fetal position-

You know you are a mother when your child throws up and you run to catch it before it hits the rug.

Suggestions for my children...if you can't be careful, you better be tough.

I am not allowed to hit snooze on my alarm clock. CPS won't let me.

"boy, *n.* 1. noise with dirt on it."

Sissy is learning to play hopscotch. All that hopping, I swear I thought I was gonna crack a hip! When did I get this old? I think I know where they got the name. First you 'hop', then you 'scotch'. Or maybe hopcabernet. :)

Baskin' in all of the lady lovin' tonight! Had a wonderful evening with old friends! (Not that they are old! That's not what I meant. They are old FRIENDS...not OLD friends. Definitely not saying they are elderly in any way. Although I am the youngest of the group, don't know if I mentioned that...how did we get here?)

Here's what just cracks me up! Have you ever seen a couple walking down the street, and at first you are thinking, "Awww, how sweet. They are going for a walk together." Then as you get closer you see that one of them has earphones on! lol "Walk with me, darling. But don't talk to me."

Dearest Kenny, my little Chesney-poo, you precious little speck of a man. Thank you for all of your little island diddies, reminding me that life is an island...or ...I'm on an island?... need to visit the islands?... don't know, anyway there were margaritas mentioned at some point. :)

Off to take Sissy to meet her preschool teacher. When she sees her teacher she says, "There she is, I think she wants to hold me." lol

Well, Bubba has spoken. After waiting patiently for his mama to finish his baby quilt (I know, he's no longer a baby...what's your point?...I've been busy!) he has adopted the coffee tablerunner. Out of desperation he has resorted to dragging it around. It's sad, really. I have reached a whole new level of sucking.

Mommy Law #17...you know you are D to the U N, DUN, when you find yourself blowing bubbles with the kids and the mother-lovin' bubbles follow you everywhere and it MAKES. YOU. CRAAAAAAZY. Blow to the left, here they come. Blow to the right, here they come! SOMEONE PLEASE TELL ME how the wind is blowing in BOTH DIRECTIONS!?! Is it bedtime yet? :/

Howard The Translator has just informed me that Jamba is Spanish for juice. You're welcome. Sleep well tonight.

Here's what you don't want...walking into your baby's room in the morning to find him looking like Elvis with his jammies unzipped down to his feet...little weenus blowin' in the breeze cuz he's removed his diaper and thrown it across the room like a monkey. Shit has LITERALLY hit the fan. And OMG, what's that SMELL???? That would be about four pounds of shizzle that is all over him...his bed... his floor...his FACE. No, you definitely don't want THAT. Welcome to Motherhood and have a nice day.

I have spent the morning downloading upgrades and upgrading downloads. Verifying upgrades and analyzing verifications. I've got software, hardware and firmware, yet still find myself with nothing TO wear. Oh, and I almost forgot...authenticating verifications because HEAVEN KNOWS you don't want to verify something that isn't authentic! Am I right?!! And don't forget the syncing! MY GOD, THE SYNCING!

I was at the new Super Target today, enjoying all of their treasures, when some scrunchies caught my eye. There were two women in the aisle, and in embarrassment I said, "I can't believe I'm actually reaching for scrunchies!" smile smile, laugh laugh...and then I saw it...one of them was WEARING. A. SCRUNCHIE. There was no recovering from this. ~blink...blink~ I dropped my scrunchie and walked away.

Why on EARTH did I walk this child to school today?! Hotter than a two dollar pistol. Ugh. #sweatrunningdownthecrackofmyass

Bubba is crying in his bed, "I fryyying, Mama! I FRYYYYYYYYYYYINGGGGGG!!" Really? Because I had no clue that this freakin' headache was from your non-stop crying. SERENITY NOW!!!!

When tidying up the house, here's a few things I've learned...that a plastic hot dog is no match for an Oreck vacuum, and a Zsu Zsu Pet will work to dust a table in a pinch. :) You're welcome.

It's my body and I'll cry if I want to.

I get so tired of repeating myself! But I guess it is like the old saying goes, writing is re-writing...peating is repeating...folding is refolding...and mothering is... exhausting.

There is a phenomenon in my house known as "Mother Butt". Without fail, as soon as Mama's butt hits the chair to eat or rest, as SOON as she lets out a heavy sigh, it signals the offspring to jump into action and all hell breaks loose. Someone spills something, falls down, or craps themselves. Without fail. Sheesh. So up again I go. MOTHERBUTTER!!! It's not a sexy life, but it's all mine. #jealousmuch

Want more? Visit Shari's blog at
www.dontmakemecounttothree.com
or look for
Tales From The Pantry: Random Rants & Musings of a Stay-At-Home Mom on Facebook!

Acknowledgements

I would like to thank my Facebook family for all of their encouragement to write this book. For all of you who lol'd and giggled along with me while I flew my dork flag high and proud, I salute you. You gave me the idea and I've enjoyed every minute. To all of my sisters at MisfitMoms.com, I believe all of the hours I've logged with you in the past six years have really helped me hone my skills and showed me that I have a love for writing and telling stories. Without you, I wouldn't be here. To my hubby, for giving me the time I needed to write and for taking on the madness in my absence. I love you. To all of the staff at Estep & Fitzgerald Publishing, you paved the way and got me where I needed to go. I am forever grateful. And to my dear friend Amy, there are no words. Your wisdom and encouragement, long hours, and counsel, are what put this book together. I couldn't have done this without you. Love you, girl!

Shari Owen Brown is a married, stay-at-home mom of two young children. She lives in a small town in Southern California. This is her first book.

ESTEP & FITZGERALD
LITERARY PUBLISHING